INDUSTRIAL AMERICA

ITS WAY OF WORK AND THOUGHT

"Man the master and servant of the Machine, harnessing to his will the forces of the material world, mechanizing labor and adding thereto the promise of leisure"

(*Mural by Frank Brangwyn, R.A., in Rockefeller Center, New York*)

☆

Industrial America

ITS WAY OF WORK AND THOUGHT

BY

ARTHUR POUND

WITH ILLUSTRATIONS

BOSTON

LITTLE, BROWN, AND COMPANY *PUBLISHERS*

1936

THE ATLANTIC MONTHLY PRESS BOOKS
ARE PUBLISHED BY
LITTLE, BROWN, AND COMPANY
IN ASSOCIATION WITH
THE ATLANTIC MONTHLY COMPANY

PRINTED IN THE UNITED STATES OF AMERICA

The individual chapters composing this volume were published originally as a series in the *Atlantic Monthly* in coöperation with the twelve corporations selected for case-studies by Mr. Pound. Every assistance has been given Mr. Pound by the staffs of these corporations in collecting his material and in verifying his facts. His series of interpretations therefore have the distinction of being in each instance authenticated at the original source.

CONTENTS

ILLUSTRATIONS

INTRODUCTION
MEN IN INDUSTRY

MEN IN INDUSTRY

In presenting twelve studies of as many large American corporations, each a leader in its field, the *Atlantic Monthly* felt that it was contributing substantially to economic recovery and to the return of confidence in the basic industries of the country. Manifestly it would not be enough to feed those in distress because of urban unemployment and to subsidize farm operations in the interest of higher prices. These aids could not be other than temporary palliatives unless, and until, industrial activity came to the rescue by relieving unemployment and increasing urban power to purchase farm products at fair price levels. A larger public understanding of corporation policies and practices would hasten these movements toward equilibrium.

On the way to this better understanding, definite questions presented themselves. What steps had industry taken to improve its processes? How far was industry fortifying itself in public esteem by lowering prices? What steps had it taken to cushion the shock of the depression for its employees? How well were its pension and insurance and savings plans working for employee benefits? How were large employers reacting to the new legislation aimed at control of wage relations and the standardization of prices? What promise could industrial research hold out for future boons through lower prices, new and better goods? In short, what is the way of work and thought of the huge fabricating and distributing groups which have become most important factors in our economic scene?

The picture might have been presented by any one of several methods. A survey might have been attempted in general terms, but that would have lacked definiteness, a fault common to most literary interpretations of industry, which itself stands and grows by being entirely definite. Consequently it was decided to take twelve outstanding leaders in what may be broadly termed the fabricating field of industry and, with the assistance of their staffs, to present a more authoritative view of their operations and policies than would have been possible without their assistance. Also, in order to round out the picture, it seemed best to concentrate attention in each case on one major aspect of corporate activity, a treatment necessary in view of the circumscribed length of the articles.

Each of these twelve corporations engages in a bewildering variety of integrated functions, some of which are little comprehended by the public. United States Steel, Johns-Manville, and Norton conduct mining as well as fabricating operations. Standard Oil (New Jersey) operates the world's largest fleet of merchant ships. General Mills and National Dairy mean tremendously much to the wheat and milk farmers of the country, and are developing new medicinal products from these great staples. In connection with its paper making, Kimberly-Clark conducts vast lumbering operations. Steel, Libbey-Owens-Ford, Norton, Johns-Manville, and Goodyear are vital elements in the automobile industry, which in a sense conditions all American large-scale business. Continental Can's story reveals the rise of the packaging industry, which has revolutionized both retail trade and dietary habits. General Motors and General Electric represent the highest efficiency yet reached in the fabrication and assembly of intricate machines for common use, through which the daily and household life of the masses has been transformed.

Some of these companies are widely owned by hundreds of thousands of stockholders; others are owned by small groups, chiefly managers and descendants of founders. Some have a high degree of centralization, others of decentralization. But, amid all their differences, certain likenesses appear. All conduct scientific research on a scale which the public little appreciates. Amid the hurly-burly of competition, each is trying to organize its activities for the long pull as well as for present profits. Each is concerned with the equities and ethics of business. Actually every great corporation, though legally a bloodless and soulless fiction, is a complex group of personalities carrying on intricate daily business under tremendous responsibilities, trying to widen its markets by giving consumers more and more for their dollars, and striving to perpetuate itself by forward plans and policies. All realize that they rise or fall, survive or perish, by performing necessary services in a way and at a price to deserve public good will, since it is to the public that they must look for capital, sales, and profits.

For economy in manufacturing and distribution over a vast territory, the modern, large-scale corporation is unbeatable. Its profits accrue from small margins on multitudinous transactions; its services are the result of minute division of labor, operating tools and systems which create ever-increasing value and service with least labor. The discipline of such corporations, and the morale flowing from that discipline, are frequently notable. They are large because the market is large, the nation broad and populous, its communications and transportation system effective. To ask if big business is too big is the equivalent of asking if the United States is too large, too well knit together, too well organized.

And yet this question, and scores of others more sternly phrased, are always being shouted at big business. Big business has been under fire in this country ever since the first stagecoach companies were organized. The chorus of criticism dies down a little during flush times, to rise again during bad times. When the public grows distressed and depressed, it hearkens to politicians who appeal to its black mood by hitting at conspicuous examples of commercial success. In these disputatious intervals it is not enough for a corporation to demonstrate that it has reduced the price of necessary goods and services far below levels ruling when business units were small, or that in employment and wages it is more just and fair than is usual in present-day small business. As an individual, a man may give his approval to big business, preferring employment by a large company to that in a small enterprise, lending a large company his money at a cheaper rate than he will lend it to an individual or a small business. Usually, too, he will find sound economic reasons for trading with large enterprises rather than with small ones. But, as psychologists who have explored the crowd spirit know full well, these individual judgments do not always carry over into the political field, and so we periodically find ourselves talking and legislating as if small businesses possessed some mystical advantages over bigness.

Now it may very well be that smallness does possess certain business advantages, but when these appear they are of a practical nature and not susceptible of accomplishment by legislative design. Businesses, like empires, may grow too fast and too large, develop bureaucratic tendencies, become inflexible and unwieldy, generate dry rot from within, neglect the morale of their personnel, and so decline. Mere size is no guarantee of future solvency, no complete insurance against disaster. The test, however, should be pragmatic rather than dictatorial, economic rather than political, arising out of events rather than out of laws or edicts. To paraphrase Aristotle, big business is good if it works and only good if it works; and a nation which keeps the lists of competition open, so that big business is always under pressure to retain its markets, need not fear that any commercial group will grow far beyond the limits set by its power to produce services.

All of us can see that the scope of effective economic coöperation is broadening. The individual operator is almost a thing of the past except in agriculture and small retail trade; the partnership, once dominant, has almost disappeared; and corporations have grown tremendously in scope and responsibilities until it is now impossible to discuss American industry intelligently without reference to the corporate form of organization. It is idle to expect the progression to stop here. The cartel trend is growing, and even nations committed to private enterprise at home are coming to direct foreign trade with increasing strictness, though perhaps not to any lasting benefit for their peoples. At the long last, something like complete regimentation may descend even upon America. But for the present, and in my opinion for generations to come, it seems that our native desire for individual advancement and our genius for voluntary coöperation will combine to keep the state from becoming more than a regulatory body in economic affairs. Whatever may be the case elsewhere, our skill in conducting private business is matched only by our lack of skill in conducting public business. And whenever our government tries a new adventure in commerce its method is to set up a government corporation as if there were magic in the name, whereas, obviously, the essence of the corporation is private enterprise to gain public favor.

Of course, advocates of more and more regulations are forever maintaining that industry creates problems which the sovereign state must undertake to solve lest the people perish. There is something to be said for that contention; by making the results of inventions and scientific processes available in increasing tempo and quantity, industry does tend to keep social life from settling into entirely safe and secure patterns. Unquestionably industry presents more boons and opportunities to an alert and able minority than to the more inert and commonplace majority, though the latter shares materially, none the less, on the consuming end by getting more for its money. But industry's rôle in unsettling social life is certainly no greater than the part played therein by its chief critic, government. Nothing quite equals war as a breeder of public ills and sorrows; yet foreign affairs and war are both government monopolies. Attempts to make industry the scapegoat for all our recent distresses fall rather flat when one recalls the part played by the Great War in increasing public debts and taxes, inflating values, and unsettling the people. The difference is that industry has to pay for its own blunders and those of government as well. A tour of American industry forces the conclusion that life would be measurably improved if city streets were as clean as factories, if international gatherings were as peaceful as trade conventions, if public electorates were as sensible as stockholder electorates, if governments were as efficient and inexpensive as business administrations.

I have been observing the evolution of American business for nearly thirty years, now inside, now outside, yet always alive to the fact that its importance in the social scheme far outran the business man's view of his job at any given moment. But progressively, through these years, business has been gaining on its critics who were wont to cite against it undue concern for present profits, callousness toward labor, and blindness in social relations. There has been a vital change in all these directions. In my youth the typical large employer held a tsarist attitude toward his help, fought bitterly against his competitors, and feared only his bankers. Rough and ready, he had risen from the ranks by sheer driving power, and in general, though with conspicuous exceptions, he proved the truth of the poet's warning to labor to beware the boss who came up in shirt sleeves. Such as he was, he was equal to his times, but his times were rough and reckless. That type has passed, as business has become progressively more scientific, better-mannered, more firmly based.

To-day business is led, not by bluff captains of industry, but by educated men accustomed to looking on all sides of the complex problems presented to them. They do not underestimate their responsibilities to stockholders, but on the other hand they realize equally other responsibilities. They accept the fact that their employees have a stake in their enterprises; they meet their men when and as occasion demands, not as enemies, but as coöperators. With full and liquid treasuries they can get working capital on easy terms from the stock-buying public; if they borrow from banks for temporary movements they "hire" the money as scientifically as an experienced family man rents a house; the banker influence in industry grows less and less. Industrial thought turns more and more toward two goals, neither of which is directly connected with prices or goods. The first is the internal organization of the business so that all the human beings in it will work harmoniously together, each developing his or her highest powers; the second is cultivating public good will at every point in the manufacturing and distributing process, from the acquisition of raw material to assuring its satisfactory use by customers. Ever more important in this process becomes advertising, with its twin, publicity. In all their aspects, corporations daily grow more public-minded, more scientific-minded, more personnel-minded.

This trend may be readily followed by reference to corporate leadership. The beginnings of any big business are usually to be traced back to some outstanding personality of the entrepreneur type. Such men had the tremendous personal force necessary to marshal capital and labor toward new objectives, or to extend the boundaries of their businesses faster and farther than their competitors. Except along the main line of their experience, the old-time leaders might be a little vague; the master manufacturer might be weak in salesmanship, and the master salesman weak in operations, the master promoter weak in finance. But the times were with them, their courage was undaunted, and they pulled by main strength through crises which undid many of their competitors.

Then, here and there in industry, bankers began to appear in positions of industrial authority, as they had hitherto appeared in railroad affairs. In the main theirs were rescue missions, and rarely lasted after financial stress ended. Next, as corporate relationships grew in complexity through mergers and as the public aspect seemed more important, lawyers came into industrial leadership, a most significant turn. The lawyer is essentially a public man, with definite responsibilities to the administration of justice and schooled in the arts of compromise. His arrival on the industrial scene could mean only that some of the heats and uncertainties of business had been eliminated. Such was, indeed, the case. Financing the problems of goods production had become secondary. Competent technical and engineering assistants could assure a steady stream of standardized and ever-improving merchandise, while impersonal capital could be secured through stock and bond markets, as long as reasonable dividends held and good prospects continued. No longer was it necessary for a corporation head to run to bankers for relief or to pay too much attention to the whims of individual stockholders; in fact, the roster of stockholders changed from day to day as shares were bought and sold. Diversity of ownership brought release, not from the responsibilities for sound management and adequate returns, but from personal influences and clique actions.

The result was that a lawyer president, often himself only a relatively small stockholder, could continue to follow his natural bent to a very considerable degree in corporate administration. His decisions were logical, considered utterances rather than snap judgments based upon personal experience or the enthusiasm of the moment. He could see that leadership held those elements of trusteeship to which he had been accustomed. Three responsibilities to three groups rested on him — a primary responsibility to the ever-changing group of stockholders whose property he was administering; a second responsibility to the employees, management and labor, without whose loyal and intelligent coöperation the properties could produce little of value; and third, to the market which absorbed his company's products and poured back into its treasury the wherewithal to maintain and enlarge the properties, to pay wages and dividends.

Customer interest could be rewarded by reduced prices and improved services. Consider how thoroughly this has been done in the fields most susceptible to mass production and improved use.   Better automobiles can be bought for twenty-five cents a pound than could be bought for two dollars a pound twenty years ago.   Ten cents will buy a better electric lamp than a dollar would buy in the early stages of the electric industry.   Many synthetic and refined compounds, once almost as costly as precious stones, can be bought to-day for less than the expense of digging inferior natural compounds from the ground.   In a very real sense, these reductions in prices and improvements in quality are consumers' dividends derived from increasing industrial efficiency.   However, in reducing prices the industrialist must step warily, weighing the prospects of increased use against costs, and considering the possibility of decreasing costs through increasing production.

Raising wages also contains elements of uncertainty. Under the ordinary conditions of land ownership in America, any sudden rise in wages for a large body of localized employees is almost certain to bring in its train a rise in rents and in the prices of necessary goods, as increased store rents become reflected in merchants' costs.   The result is that a considerable proportion of any payroll increase eventually becomes diverted to landlords.   This explains, I think, many aspects of those corporate activities which are frequently criticized as paternalistic, including housing projects, welfare work, mutual insurance, aid to savings, and other forms of off-the-payroll remuneration.

It would be simpler, by far, for a corporation to disburse the cost of these aids in cash, but in that case the prospect of real betterment to employees would be lessened.   Here must be considered also the inexperience of employees in conserving and investing funds, the stake of their wives and children in the pay envelope, and the community interest, which is often best served by the corporation's providing facilities for recreation, education, and medical care which could hardly be maintained on a strictly individualist basis. This is especially true in small cities and towns where the industry involved is the major, or perhaps the sole, economic prop of the community.   In general, it is hardly feasible for any corporation to pay wages greatly in excess of the going rate for the community for the same kind of work, since marked disturbance in the economic balance of any section usually brings compensating reactions in the cost of living.

By no means were all of these off-the-payroll boons to labor delivered by lawyers come to industrial authority. Some of them actually were, however, and these penetrated by example sufficiently far to make the lawyer contribution significant.   Also, and this is important, the lawyers were able to make both their own moves and those of others articulate and understandable to wide audiences eager for light on social and industrial relations.   It may be said that the legal influence introduced the idea of justice, the habit of compromise, and the institutional idea into American industry.   Lawyer chiefs were more open than their more practical predecessors had been to the waves of opinion which were blowing through the world of affairs.   Hence they absorbed and applied to their groups, with appropriate reservations, many of the social ideals propounded by men of larger vision but less experience.   To some extent they founded, and to a greater extent they codified and reën- forced, the precedents taken over by the next group of industrial leaders to appear on the scene.

For new times, new men.   Whenever, for one reason or another, any one aspect of industry becomes outstandingly important, men skilled in that aspect of business will rise to authority. We have seen how the master manufacturer and the master promoter gave way, in some important industries, to banker leaders in financial pinches, and to lawyer leaders following mergers which created involved contractual relations calling for judicial poise in harmonizing a corporation's internal affairs and skill in presenting its case to the public. Then in the twenties, when technical advances based on scientific research had gained fresh recognition as a result of the World War and when the nation appeared to have accepted corporate prosperity as part and parcel of its own well-being, technical men rose swiftly to leadership. It is significant that two thirds of the heads of the businesses presented in this series have had scientific and technical training in universities or colleges. They advanced to power in an era which set high value on competent operating men, when volume production was in demand, when there seemed no limit to benefits of increasing productivity per man-hour through every possible labor-saving device, division of labor, and specialization of talent. Trained men of this effective type buried the world in goods till it could scarcely breathe; but are they to be blamed because the distributional facilities of society are so primitive that it could not manage itself under plenty? I do not think so. Society will have to catch up with its engineers and scientists, for the latter are certain to keep traveling toward their destined and worthy goal — the satisfaction of human wants with the least effort.

In stressing this change of emphasis, let no easy inference be made that corporate interest in employee relations and public good will declined under enhanced technical efficiency. Rather, the former became in a sense standard practice, to be handled by subordinate staffs of experts instead of by the head of the company, improvising as he felt his way

gingerly along.   In the meantime, underbrush had been
cleared away, objectives visualized, policies clarified, procedure organized.   Advertising, publicity, public relations,
employee representation, rose to new heights from firm
bases.   What had been somewhat of a personal adventure,
perhaps even a hobby, of the boss became the orderly business of a group.   Industry overlooked no avenue for
presenting to public consideration, not only its goods and
services, but also its thought patterns and policies.

As one travels America acquainting himself with industries
of various kinds and backgrounds, he grows aware of the
influences of materials and environments on all the groupings of man, including the most efficient of those groupings,
the corporation.   There are subtle differences in the business atmosphere of New York, Pittsburgh, Toledo, Chicago,
Omaha.   There are vital, impressive differences in tempo
between an industrial corporation which calmly and methodically draws from the earth a natural resource, and processes
and delivers an utterly necessary commodity which mankind
will accept without reference to style, — such as oil or steel,
— and another corporation functioning under the inexorable
lash of fashion.   The first proceeds deliberately, almost
majestically, on its way;   the second is characteristically
harried and hurried, torn between desire to be first in the
field with an innovation and an equally strong desire to
test every phase of the novelty before it risks presentation.
Age, too, conditions a corporation;   you will find new
corporations still wrestling internally over matters which
older ones have reduced to effective routine.

Corporations reflect the personalities of their founders
and the circumstances of their founding; with them certain
ways of thinking and doing have been reduced to habit,
backed by the weight of tradition.   In one, the route to

the top may be won only through long service, while another searches for new blood when it determines on a change. One board of directors may be small and composed of men who have spent their lives in the business and have risen from the ranks, while another board may be three or four times as large and include members drawn from other activities. A large board is apt to be a ratifying rather than a directing body, vital direction coming from an executive committee of the board. At one corporate address, directors will be found in session at a regular hour on nearly every business day; at another, they will gather only at stated intervals, and then somewhat formally and ceremoniously. In general, however, directors are doing more directing in American corporations than they did of old, although management still gets a rather free hand, as is entirely natural in a youthful society and in fields of action where speed counts.

The stockholder, in corporations whose shares are widely scattered, receives rather comprehensive printed reports, but, unless his holdings are large, must be content with little personal attention. The American way is to pay the stockholder well, to treat him honestly and gently, but to keep him in his place, so that he has neither the desire nor the extended opportunity to interfere with operations and policies. This is the inevitable result of dividing ownership among many thousands of persons, and beyond question is one of the factors contributing to corporate energies in the United States. When not abused, — and the companies represented in this series have been careful not to abuse it, — this attitude, with general acceptance of it, makes directly for stability in corporate affairs and gives scope for long-range planning. If stockholder voting were as emotional a process as the electoral process in politics, corporate planning would be as unlikely to succeed as government planning. Within limits, the divorcement of capital from managerial responsibility seems to possess more advantages than disadvantages. A busy public wants dividends rather than responsibilities, and if a corporate management is thoroughly trusted it is frequently able to go to rather extraordinary lengths in using company funds for employee and community purposes without arousing stockholder protest, and even with hearty stockholder approval. So impersonal has finance grown that to-day it makes little difference who owns a corporation and a great deal of difference who operates it. A proved management to-day has less trouble on the capital end than it has on the labor end, a complete reversal of the situation existing thirty or forty years ago. In our restless, dynamic manner we Americans have solved certain equations in economics; we have mastered scarcity both as to goods and as to capital needed for goods production; but steady distribution of goods, and security through maintained purchasing power for farmers and wage earners, are still beyond us.

In *The Iron Man in Industry*, published in 1921, I drew a rough comparison between the dukedom in the mediæval world and the great corporation in the present. Subsequent evolution of the corporation has strengthened the analogy. Both operate, though not always comfortably, under the sovereign. The one largely directed the minutiæ of social life in the past, the other does so in the present. Like the dukedom, the corporation has become the chief financial support of the state, not only through the taxes it pays directly, but also through the taxable income it distributes as dividends and its payrolls, which are the true economic base of the taxable incomes of local landlords and traders. In the Middle Ages he who lived under a just and able duke was lucky; so to-day he is lucky who lives under a just and able corporation. Under such discipline — and there be few among us who do not need discipline — the average man reaches perhaps his highest effectiveness. One must never expect a perfect coördination in human affairs; and in a world where family and college discords are not unknown it is idle to expect complete harmony in corporate relations. But under the corporate form of organization have evolved the most effective ways and means yet discovered to bring large numbers of persons together in wealth production.

Government cannot match corporate industry in either celerity or elasticity of effort. Armies under fear of death, nerved by crisis, and inspired by an outstanding personality, may coöperate more efficiently for a short pull, but armies do not pay their way. Instead, they draw for support on the savings of the past and the earnings of the future. At the other extreme of government action stands a government bureau, its members secure against dismissal and without hope of early recognition and reward, slogging along dutifully year after year on routine tasks. But a bureaucracy does not pay its way, either. The sinews for both war and government come from the wealth makers, those who work with mind and hand, using the aids of capital and science. The latter reach their most fruitful union in modern industry, corporately organized, but finding more and more room inside its legal mould for the group satisfactions and loyalties which flourish in the fertile soil of industrial competence.

PRECISION AND PERSPECTIVE

General Motors' Philosophy of Industrial Progress

I

PRECISION AND PERSPECTIVE

WHEN the only records of discovery were myths passed along in folklore, the Greeks credited their hero, Prometheus, with stealing fire from heaven for his fellow mortals, and gave to Demeter, goddess of agriculture and fertility, praise for easing the toil of her earth-bound sons by granting them the wheel, greatest of labor-saving tools. Ever since those mists of antiquity dissolved, the most important business of mankind has been that of joining the gifts of Prometheus and Demeter by putting the power of fire behind wheels. The very pace of life depends upon the speed with which matter can be changed into energy available for transport.

Of old, the key men in transportation were stock breeders and coach makers; then inventors of steam engines and railroad builders. Now they are scientists and automotive engineers. The former discover ways and means of increasing the energy applied to wheels; the latter adapt these discoveries by balancing the ideal against the practical to improve motor cars. Like the composer of a symphony, the engineer must be aware of the myriad possibilities and limitations of the elements in his ensemble. The result of ever-improving engineering, which flows from the sense of proportion firmly held by large staffs of carefully selected specialists, is that most widely used of modern mechanisms — the gasoline motor car.

On this base has arisen almost within a generation an industry of world-wide influence, under whose impetus material progress for the masses has been accelerated faster than ever before. The achievements of yesterday or to-day outrun in meaning those of many a distant century. This industry is overwhelmingly American both in production and in point of view. Of the 33,330,000 automobiles used in the world in 1933, 72 per cent were owned in the United States. Even in that slack year nearly 2,000,000 passenger cars and trucks, worth approximately $1,000,000,000, were manufactured in the United States, of which nearly one eighth were exported. In the banner year of 1929, total United States and Canadian production reached 5,621,715 units, worth more than $3,500,000,000.

This output absorbs so much of America's basic production that automobile manufacture is the nation's key industry. It is the largest buyer of steel, rubber, plate glass, nickel, lead, mohair, upholstery leather, and malleable iron, and a heavy consumer of lumber, aluminum, copper, and tin. Automotive employment in all lines exceeds 3,000,000 persons, and indirectly another 1,500,000. When you buy an automobile, scores of industries and technical arts divide the proceeds.

In this pivotal industry General Motors occupies a central position. It manufactures and sells every year through its five car divisions — Chevrolet, Pontiac, Oldsmobile, Buick, and Cadillac-LaSalle, as well as General Motors Truck — approximately 40 per cent of all passenger cars and trucks manufactured in the United States. This volume of trade alone makes it one of the world's most impressive businesses, of interest to everyone who desires to know how a large industry functions in arriving at commercial eminence. But General Motors has other aspects even more significant than size and success. Unlike many other great companies, its eggs are not all in one basket.

It takes to market a wide array of products other than motor cars and their accessories, among them many household appliances. The most widely used of these is Frigidaire, the first electric refrigerator to reach quantity production, giving rise to successful developments in air-conditioning systems, for domestic and commercial use, sold under the same trade name. Another well-known name is that of Delco, applied to a wide range of electrical products for household, farm, and accessory uses. These stem back to the former Dayton Engineering Laboratories Company, forerunner of the present General Motors Research Division.

The seeds of scientific research will flower in many different forms; in the case of General Motors the developments are naturally associated with motor power. This explains the diversity of General Motors, a diversity which ranges from giant Diesels to tiny Durex bearings, from airplanes to household appliances. The need for precision in this variety of highly specialized products, together with emphasis upon the open mind in scientific research and engineering practice, has moved General Motors toward a balanced and steady point of view which is now its chief characteristic. This appears, as we shall see, in fields apparently remote from the engineering influence. Precision, ever more demanding through the years, in designing and manufacturing motor cars, has helped to create a perspective now dominant in all General Motors affairs.

The first gasoline engines were perhaps 5 per cent efficient; yet even these ranked high in contrast with steam engines. To-day the best ones are 30 per cent efficient and the efficiency ratio is steadily rising. Ethyl gasoline, developed by General Motors, played a very important part in this gain. But engineers and technicians still have plenty of leeway this side of perfection in recovering for public use the high potential energy of gasoline. The man behind the automobile wheel seldom realizes that he is using a fuel six times as powerful as nitroglycerine. With all its faults, faults more apparent to the specialist than to the layman, the automobile engine even in inexpert hands is several times more efficient than a steam engine in expert hands.

Significant socially is the fact that the owner-operator of a gasoline car is also the citizen who votes and pays for good roads and other traffic accommodations. America has been gaining a new landscape. Extension of hard-surfaced roads, broadening of urban, suburban, and country-side developments, centralized schools, and scores of other changes equally obvious and momentous, all result from social pressure to adjust the American scene to public desire for the fullest possible satisfaction from its favorite con-veyance. Anyone who glances at the list of automobile references in the index to *Recent Social Trends* must be impressed by its massive testimony to the automobile's influence on rural, community, family, church, and economic life. The American point of view has changed along with its landscape. We are not as sectional as we were, nor as stand-pat. We know that there is another side to every hill and depend largely upon scientific and industrial ad-vance to push us over the top.

The safety of the motoring population, no less than its convenience and satisfaction, is an essential which auto-mobile engineers jealously guard. It is easy for any smart engineer to exaggerate any characteristic of a car along almost any line. In fact, this is not nearly so difficult as wise design based upon proper correlation of the factors necessary to economy, safety, durability, ease of operation, style appeal, and riding quality, to mention only a few.

Emphasis on one feature of performance may be at the expense of other features.

Many an ideal gain must wait until a way can be found to incorporate it in the car without disturbing the existing balance of forces and materials. Perhaps a new alloy is needed. The engineer must often mark time for the metallurgist, and the metallurgist for the chemist. The influences of the scientist, the technician, and the consumer meet in the engineering rooms, where through twenty-five years there has been evolving a balanced practice and philosophy of engineering advance.

At its birth in 1908, General Motors gathered together a number of automobile and parts companies, each independently operated. One of these, Olds Motor Works, erected the first American factory for automobile production. It pioneered in modern assembly methods and, in its famous Oldsmobile runabout, first reached quantity production. Another, Cadillac, had just won the Dewar trophy in London for the greatest contribution to automobile advance, by demonstrating the interchangeability of parts which is the key to the assembly line and to mass production. This naturally stressed higher engineering standards.

General Motors realized early that every model must be an engineering unit, planned from inception to carry a certain load, with each part designed in relation to all other parts. In an industry rapidly advancing both in machine shop practice and in scientific research, the less left to chance and whim the better. The process was one of reducing complications for users, at the price of increasing complications of engineering. Concern for customer peace of mind brought to pass a situation which would be considered remarkable if it were not commonplace. To-day

the automobile buyer acquires at reasonable cost one of
the most complicated machines ever devised by human
ingenuity.   He operates that machine without being aware
precisely what mechanical and chemical processes he controls.

This engineering progress, by enhancing the personal
mobility of millions, inevitably brought the great public
into the automobile orbit.   There began to develop, within
an organization accustomed to the working out of precise
relationships, a growing recognition of the manifold equities
involved in its rapidly expanding business.   Here again
the sense of proportion, the feeling that General Motors
was in business for the long pull, made itself effective.   In
its major relations General Motors arrived at a code of
its own years before the word "code" became a commonplace in industry.   Its leaders perceived that in the long
run General Motors would survive through the equitable
nature of its dealings with certain large groups whose good
will was essential.   To stockholders it owed reasonable
dividends and security; to suppliers it owed fair prices; to
employees it owed good wages and salaries which would
maintain a high purchasing power; to dealers it owed opportunity for fair profits; to customers it owed dependable
merchandise and satisfactory service; and to the American
people it owed such an administration of its affairs that
it could never be justly accused of lack of candor or dis-
regard of public interest.

Indication of the wisdom of this policy may be seen in
a stockholder list of some 350,000 names.   General Motors
rejoices in this evidence of public confidence.   Such a
large stockholder interest gives news value to all General
Motors announcements and financial statements.   These
are notable for their frank and detailed character, as befits

ALFRED P. SLOAN, JR.
President, General Motors Corporation

Motor assembly line in the Olds plant of General Motors

an accounting rendered to thousands of persons with small stock holdings unaccustomed to interpreting condensed financial statements. Such trends and activities have led General Motors to think of and conduct itself as "a public-minded institution."

These policies have borne results. Preferred stock dividends have been paid regularly, and only once since common dividends began have they been interrupted. When hours of work had to be reduced in the plants, a programme of work sharing was promptly inaugurated. The sum of $97,000,000 became available to participating employees from 1930 to 1933 inclusive through withdrawals from Savings and Investment Funds, accumulated through prosperous years as the joint result of individual thrift and company participation. When the Michigan banking troubles of 1933 left Detroit without a large commercial bank, General Motors joined with the Federal Government to establish the National Bank of Detroit. This it did entirely without hope of profit or expectation of remaining in the banking business, and thereby provided facilities for ordinary trade and industry in that community. At the first possible moment wages were advanced to pre-depression levels and in some cases beyond, while complete coöperation was given to the government in raising employment by shortening hours in accordance with code provisions. Recently the management has set up adequate machinery for resolving labor disputes through conference with freely elected representatives of its workers. The plan has been carefully considered and fits in with the traditions of a body of labor which was drawn into an expanding and high-wage industry largely from the fields and forests of Michigan, a population individualist by nature and traditionally more alive to personal opportunity than to collective action.

This far-sighted plan is the considered utterance of men who do not promise lightly.

From a survey of these developments, all the way from engineering and factory details up to the matters of broad social import, there emerge the outlines of a corporate character in which the dominant note is a well-balanced sense of proportion. General Motors avoids "trick" engineering and flashy financing, because it expects to be in business a long time. It cannot afford to hurry unduly a hopeful development; it can afford to wait until it is sure that every contingency has been foreseen by trained minds.

In bringing the automobile thus far along, epoch-making changes, which seem to come like lightning, are usually the fruitage of patient years of study. Such was Charles F. Kettering's Delco electric self-starter, in the days of the Dayton Engineering Laboratories Company. This great innovation was in the making for years before it became standard equipment on Cadillac in 1912. Again, although rear-wheel braking had developed an impressive body of brake knowledge by 1923, several months were required by Buick to work that knowledge over effectively enough to warrant the pioneer installation of four-wheel brakes. Engineers were aware that fitting brakes to front wheels involved an entirely new set of factors. This became a decisive achievement, since the new braking system, instead of being merely added, had been incorporated in the car with attention to every necessary chassis alteration. Still a third case is independent front-wheel suspension, popularly known as "knee-action" wheels. All new mechanical developments are rigorously tested at the 1248-acre General Motors Proving Ground, where every kind of terrain and driving surface is represented.

While divisional autonomy prevails in General Motors engineering practice, it is the special function of the Research Laboratories and the central engineering staff to conduct added studies along original lines, presenting the results to divisional staffs; to undertake tests and studies at the request of divisional staffs; and to advise with divisional staffs. Within this broad control final responsibility rests with the divisional engineers. They stand or fall by their products, and no limits are set upon their resourcefulness within the limits of sound practice. Standardization of materials is emphasized throughout; but standardization of thought — No!

For the sake of convenience and economy certain material specifications, such as screw threads, have been standardized; but in the realm of ideas and methods the emphasis is all on the open mind, not only as to specific improvements, but also as to new ways of fitting those improvements into a well-proportioned whole. Products are standardized only in the sense that for a given period a single model may be manufactured economically in quantity, but no sooner is that model in production than engineers begin the improvements which will mark its successor. Experiments are under way to-day which may be five years or more in reaching the public. When a variation has been tested market-wise by one division, it is thereafter available to all divisions. Thus, as in the case of the electric self-starter, crank-case ventilation, and synchro-mesh transmission, the step may first be taken on Cadillac, the highest-priced car in the line, and then applied to the less expensive cars as costs and circumstances permit. An innovation may be used first on a quantity car, as in the case of Duco lacquer finish, before being extended to other cars. Or, after thorough laboratory and Proving Ground tests, a change may be made in the general line, as was the case with both knee-action wheels and no-draft ventilation.

Fuel research provides a striking example of the untrammeled activity of the General Motors Research Division in its influence on the engineering staffs of car divisions. About fifteen years ago engineers awoke to the fact that inferior fuels were limiting engine efficiency. Endeavors to secure more power from an engine of given size were checkmated by the "knock," characteristic of the gasoline then available. Years passed before the fuel, rather than the engine design, was recognized as the culprit, after arduous scientific detective work. Thousands of compounds were burned in a cylinder under observation. Of these, several silenced the knock by delaying the burning of the last of the fuel charge, thus removing the over-high pressure due to almost instantaneous combustion. At last one such compound seemed to have commercial possibilities. This was tetraethyl lead, then expensive simply because it was produced in small quantity. A new industry, which in its present stage involves the recovery of bromine from sea water and opens possibilities of recovering other values from the treasure house of the sea, had to be developed before the result of these chemical researches could be utilized by the public.

The story of Ethyl, trade name of an anti-knock compound for mixing with gasolines, is one of the great pursuit tales of science, similar to that of Edison's search for a satisfactory electric light filament. Not the least of the achievements of Ethyl research was to raise one of the limiting factors in engine design and to set the stage for a series of improvements hitherto not feasible. Technical advances matured in this thorough way benefit General Motors and its customers directly; they also become part of the ever-growing body of knowledge which society inherits, each generation becoming richer than its predecessor in means of controlling natural forces and elevating living standards.

Many General Motors innovations increase employment through stimulating activity by suppliers of new materials; others prove decisively beneficial in great industries altogether outside of the automotive field. For instance, note the welcome accorded by practical railway executives to General Motors improvements on the Diesel engine, long manufactured by its subsidiary, the Winton Engine Corporation. Streamlined trains, the stainless-steel Burlington Zephyr and the aluminum M-10,001 of the Union Pacific, electrically driven by current generated on the train itself, have recently broken American records for sustained railway speeds on long runs. As yet their speed possibilities have not been fully attained. This stirring development, which has brought new life to railroads, was initiated by an industry generally held to be their most pressing competitor. By applying to Diesel engines the knowledge gained through concentration upon gasoline engines, General Motors came to the rescue of another transportation industry in which, for reasons not at all discreditable, large-scale research and experiment had been neglected.

Perils of leadership beset the engineer in all fields, particularly in the automotive industry. For example, General Motors assumed heavy risks when it revised the whole low-cost car situation by making Chevrolet a six-cylinder car, thereby sounding the death knell of "fours" in the passenger car field. To reëquip its factories for the enormous production which followed cost as much as the entire capitalization of some good-sized companies. The result was to give a decisive twist to automobile progress and to make Chevrolet the most popular motor car.

Looking backward, it is easy to see that every improvement in process and product by General Motors has benefited the entire industry no less than the public. The electric self-starter, which overnight doubled the potential drivers by adding women to the number, was hailed as impracticable. When Buick adopted four-wheel brakes the cry of "danger" was raised in advance of public trial. In lesser degree, but nevertheless sufficiently to emphasize the penalties of leadership, these demonstrated successes were put through the wringer of criticism — Duco, crankcase ventilation, Ethyl gasoline, tiltbeam and multibeam headlights, the intake silencer, automatic choke, and synchro-mesh transmission. More recently Fisher no-draft ventilation and individual front-wheel suspension have established themselves as features likely to enjoy long public favor. The newest contribution is the all-steel roof, or "turret top," appearing in the 1935 General Motors line.

General Motors' philosophy of business includes the conviction that the public can be trusted to reject changes which either lack merit or involve enough care and expense to offset their merits. The common sense of a mechanically-minded people soon discovers the difference between a decisive improvement and a mere "gadget." The latter may do precisely what it is intended to do. But if what it does is relatively unimportant, increases hazards, or decreases comfort, it soon dies a natural death. A recent example was the free-wheeling device, which works admirably but to no important purpose, and involves extra operating risks.

Extreme streamlining is another innovation which will probably lose its appeal gradually, although not without influencing designers toward new beauties in line with the youthful science of aerodynamics. President Alfred P. Sloan, Jr., recently analyzed the subject of streamlining of automobiles as follows: "The popular belief is that there is a very distinct gain in the general efficiency of a design embodying certain aerodynamic features. The operating conditions of these various instrumentalities of transportation [1] are so different that each must be considered on the basis of its own individual circumstances, so far as the question of efficiency is concerned. As applied to motor cars, in which General Motors is primarily interested, there are in reality no important economies in the practical sense of the word, in either first cost or operating cost. The greatest possible gain that can be expected is a somewhat higher top speed, or perhaps at top speed a slight saving in fuel, all other circumstances being the same."

In a business characterized by huge volume and high preliminary expense, innovations cost money. They are profitable when they win acceptance, burdensome when they fail. To eliminate guesswork, General Motors has undertaken to guard against marketing blunders by studying public moods and desires in advance of production. The Customer Research Staff of General Motors discovers what automotive improvements the public most desires, and passes that information on to engineering staffs.

Ingenuity of approach, thoroughness of investigation, and volume of information from all parts of the country combine to make this a unique guide to engineering policy. More than 500,000 motorists have answered the bureau's questionnaires, including 81,000 "sophisticates" with evident expert knowledge. These alert enthusiasts are eyes

[1] Airplanes and streamlined trains.

and ears for General Motors throughout the nation, reporting what they see and hear and think. Always ahead of the rank and file, they indicate what the public will be looking for in the near future. In practice, a balance must be struck between what the mass mind will accept and what the sophisticate desires.

Customer research shows that purchase of a motor car is one of the most serious decisions taken by the American citizen. Since the average automobile is replaced once in four years, John Doe may be considered as in the market only that often, his buying ardor lasting for some sixty days, during which period he expects to have his wants taken seriously. He takes counsel of his family and resents being rushed off his feet by "high-pressure" salesmen. The buying mood of to-day is sober, deliberate, and insistent on full information, an attitude which is in complete harmony with the whole General Motors point of view.

Selling has become sales engineering, a matter of calm study rather than strong argument, a business of weighing trends and giving the public what it wants.

Of course, customer recommendations do not always bear immediate results. The situation is analogous to house building, where the customer expresses desires but leaves it to the architect to incorporate the suggestions in the plan, if the budget permits and the amateur ideas are not impracticable. Customer research is thus an avenue of contact between users and designers, of value to both in the long run as a means of avoiding guesswork and snap decisions.

With all its scientific research, with all its engineering technique, with all its inquiries into customer preferences, General Motors recognizes that these would be of no avail

Giant presses at General Motors Fisher Body plant, used in forming steel tops for automobiles

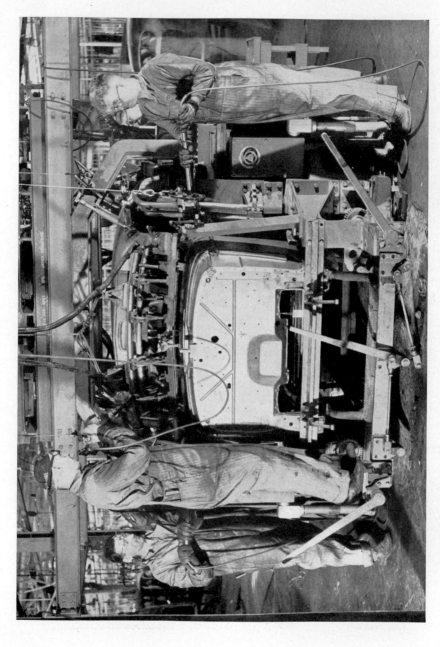

Interior of General Motors Fisher Body plant, showing body operations

except for the loyal coöperation of skilled factory employees who bring the ripe wisdom of experienced craftsmen to the solutions of problems not reducible to blueprints.

In General Motors factories one frequently hears this sentence: "Our best output is men."   And with it another: "We can do it, because we have the men."   The organization which normally employs more than 200,000 persons in its world-wide operations remembers that personnel is the foundation of the pyramid; the men who make, vend, and service the goods can break the engineer's heart and the company's reputation with the public.   Management is aware that its engineers and its factory men, working together, have built its prestige in the market place.   In both human and trade relations, as well as in the engineering progress which General Motors has made available to the public through its products, harmonious, equitable coöperation is the goal.

This, then, is General Motors, drawing on the past but looking also to the future, as indicated by its watchword, "An Eye to the Future — an Ear to the Ground."   This reflects a determination to give the public what it wants in better products year after year, and at the same time to protect consumers against questionable experiments.   In financial solidity and volume of trade General Motors ranks among the world's leading business organizations; but equally noteworthy is its growth toward policies and methods of procedure which give it survival value beyond those of inventory and balance sheet.   To these it has been led after calm fact-finding; after balancing against one another all the considerations in its complex problems, precisely as its engineers and scientists bring the open mind and a due sense of proportion to bear upon the technical problems involved in design and manufacture.

Industrial engineering has grown in this case to possess social implications. As the need for perspective has been heightened by the engineering precision which has made the motor car a commonplace in modern society, so the exact thought habits of science have been followed until perspective has been transferred to non-engineering fields and relationships in an attempt to see the responsibility of modern industry steadily and see it whole. This suggests the classic definition of the task of philosophy, "to see life steadily and see it whole." The disciplined and coöperative intelligence manifest in this vital industrial grouping is a direct result of the long schooling man has undergone all through the ages under a great and driving imperative to put power, more power and ever more power, behind wheels for the increasing convenience and prosperity of society.

CORPORATE MANAGEMENT AND EMPLOYEE WELFARE

United States Steel Shoulders a Relief Problem

II

CORPORATE MANAGEMENT AND EMPLOYEE
WELFARE

Did you ever attend a convention of organized charity? If you did, the first thing which jumped to your attention was the deep cleavage of opinion regarding the very nature of philanthropy. How far has society the right to inquire into and direct the intimate concern of those whose living conditions fall below some approved standard? And to the directors of vast corporations the same problem constantly recurs. Does their responsibility cease when they have passed a man his full wage? Is business solely a bargain between employer and employed, and has a corporation carried it out when it fills the pay envelope with the week's earnings?

Now the creation of workable conditions is often called paternalism, and paternalism has an intrusive and unpleasant sound. Call it what you will, it is not my purpose to argue the rights and wrongs of the matter, but rather to tell a chapter of history which to my thinking casts a white light upon a question that goes to the root of things. It is a chapter in the story of the United States Steel Corporation.

The example of the United States Steel Corporation is most impressive for two reasons: first, because of the large number of employees involved and the sums required to sustain them in adversity; second, because it shows a systematic programme matured for another purpose being adapted to employee relief under pressure of social adversity.

The record shows that in the pinch United States Steel aided its labor to the extent of many millions. Legally there was no compulsion to do this, but the Steel directorate firmly upheld its chairman, Mr. Myron C. Taylor, who proclaimed early in the depression that, no matter how long it might last, no employee of record would go without the necessities of life.

How had this definite point of view on employer responsibility for employee welfare been reached? The answer takes us back to the founding of the Steel Corporation in 1901. From its beginnings the steel industry had been marked by ruthless competition and hence was highly sensitive to the swings of the business cycle. Whenever hard times hit the country, the steel towns would be on short rations. In the years immediately following the inception of the Corporation, substantial progress was made in stabilizing employment. While competition continued keen between Steel and its rivals, the various subsidiaries of the Corporation were gradually brought into full coöperation. Plant specialization not only produced of itself better steel; steadier work in these specialized plants also seemed to be producing better men, who in turn made better steel.

Better men could not be held without better living conditions. That became apparent as the Corporation took over or organized activities in new quarters, such as the Mesaba range in Minnesota, the Birmingham district in Alabama, and Gary, Indiana. At many points it encountered almost frontier conditions, in which towns had to be built swiftly near natural resources. In many coal areas the Steel Corporation came into possession not only of mines but also of houses, streets, and such public services as existed. There the problem was one of improving living and health conditions for employees. Speed was one consideration; efficient correlation of plants, housing, highways, railroads, and public services was another. Either the Steel Corporation could leave this community building and rebuilding to chance and the local politicians, or it could itself proceed with the task. It elected to do the latter, in line with expert advice in town planning and the conviction that good living conditions for labor would prove a sound investment for the company.

This conviction was firmly held by Judge Elbert H. Gary, who came into the steel business in the 'nineties from the profession of law and service on the bench. As a judge he was accustomed to weighing equities, accepting fiduciary responsibilities, and thinking of himself as a trustee. In addition, Judge Gary had in him a strong leaven of the patriarch; he wanted everyone in Steel to benefit from its operations.

In the Steel equation were elements peculiar to itself. Several of these have been mentioned; another was the fact that some of its most important operations in the Pittsburgh and Chicago districts were then manned largely by foreign-born labor. Not yet fully Americanized, these men of European origin were actuated by personal thrift rather than a desire for higher living standards. Also it should be recalled that when Steel's welfare programme was initiated Judge Gary and his associates — and in fact nearly all the leaders of his day — were influenced by a sweeping public opinion in favor of welfare work as a short cut to social justice.

The welfare policy so evolved needs no apology, either as to plan or as to performance. In a project covering so large a territory and contacting so many human beings in their personal and family relationships, isolated instances of misdirected activity, friction, and unsympathetic personnel are bound to arise. To snipe at those exceptions to the rule from a safe distance is to miss the reality of the drive;

the procession marches on, in spite of the stragglers who fall out of line or the minor disputes within the ranks. In this case the procession contains more than 225,000 men and women and their dependents — a total of several million persons, if to workers and their dependents are added other residents of Steel towns who benefit directly or indirectly by Steel payrolls and the Corporation's community services.

It is worth noting that when Judge Gary asked his directors for the funds to carry on this campaign his arguments were both humanitarian and economic. This activity would pay eventually, he said, because healthy, well-disposed men did better work than half-sick, undependable, worried, or uninterested men. The world of steel is populated from top to bottom by practical men, all of whom understand that welfare, in the long run, pays its way.

Over a space of more than twenty years the Steel Corporation spent upwards of $10,000,000 a year for the welfare of its employees, and in that spirit administered the following properties as of June 30, 1934: —

25,347 dwellings and boarding houses leased to employees at low rental rates.

24 churches, the clergymen being chosen by the congregations and all business conducted under the rules usual to each denomination.

17 schools, owned, leased, or operated for apprenticeship, vocational training, and general education.

34 clubhouses, generally equipped with reading rooms, assembly and dance halls, gymnasiums, and in some cases swimming pools. Used as social centres for music and drama.

53 restaurants and lunch rooms, where meals are sold at moderate cost.

176 rest and waiting rooms.

MYRON C. TAYLOR

Chairman, Board of Directors, United States Steel Corporation

The fourth stand of the 96-inch continuous steel mill in operation
— the largest mill of this type in the world

(South Works Plant, Carnegie-Illinois Steel Corporation, South Chicago, Illinois)

120 playgrounds, many fully equipped; a large number of wading pools and swimming pools. Average attendance in summer 25,000 children daily.

17 swimming pools of large size, available for use by adults.

96 athletic fields, many of which are equipped with grandstands and with facilities for baseball, football, field events, etc.

19 practical housekeeping centres, in which American housekeeping standards are taught by demonstration. Usually used as residences for the various staffs of visiting nurses.

On the health, safety, and sanitation side the Corporation maintained : —

9 base hospitals with complete staffs and full equipment.

224 emergency stations for prompt treatment in case of accidental injuries and sudden illness.

406 company surgeons, physicians, and internes.

199 nurses, including those in training.

86 hospital orderlies and attendants.

33 visiting nurses.

24 sanitary inspectors on full time.

712 piped systems for drinking water.

628 wells and springs protected against pollution.

2452 complete comfort stations with closets, washrooms, locker facilities, etc.

5627 shower baths, available to workmen.

Steel's inventory of accommodations and services shows a concern for the bases of family and social life — housing, religion, education, public health, industrial safety, hospital care, and recreation, including music, drama, libraries, and club activities of many kinds. No corporation in the world has a more broadly conceived programme for its employees, or carries that programme forward in as many differing environments with as many kinds and conditions of employees.

As a concrete example of progress in a unique and difficult situation, the Birmingham field offers an impressive lesson. When the Tennessee Coal, Iron and Railroad Company was taken over in 1908, the Steel Corporation became the leading employer in an area obviously backward in many of the aspects of modern life. The labor force, predominantly Negro, lived within fifteen miles of Birmingham in small insanitary villages. Marshes, mosquitoes, and malaria composed a triumvirate which afflicted a population powerless to cope with that enfeebling disease. Soon after acquiring ownership, the Corporation began to construct model housing in new groupings and to remodel the houses and rearrange the streets and public services in the old villages, with running water in every house and with ample yard and garden space. The villages contain commissaries, bathhouses, schools, churches, and clubhouses constructed by the Company.

These measures did not fully meet the challenge of disease, and in 1913 a Department of Health was formed with four divisions: sanitary, medical, dental, and base hospital. The department itself was on a par with other operating departments of Tennessee Coal & Iron.

The task facing this new department was equivalent to that encountered in sanitating Limon, Costa Rica, or Guayaquil, Ecuador, engineering and medical feats which attracted world-wide attention. In extent it has been compared to the sanitating of the Panama Canal area, which preceded the successful completion of that mighty work. If the terrible toll of malaria and other filth diseases was to be reduced, an area of hundreds of square miles required close and unremitting attention, and a population unschooled in health measures had to be educated in the decencies of modern living. On the preventive side the

sanitary division undertook the following duties: to eliminate mosquitoes, ensure pure water supplies, clean and drain
streets and alleys, cut weeds and grass, collect and dispose
of trash and garbage, inspect work places and dwelling
places, supervise stables for fly control, maintain quaran-
tines for communicable diseases, and protect food supplies.

Whether those communities, some of which had little or
no voting strength because the population was mostly
colored, would ever have sanitated themselves is a question
for which the practical answer is this: they had not done
so and showed no intention of doing so. Either the Company must do the job, or there was little prospect that it
would be done within any reasonable period. The task
was not only beyond the grasp of those communities as an
idea; it was also beyond their financial and scientific resources.

Consider, for instance, the elements involved in the
campaign against mosquitoes, to take only one of the sanitary division's triumphs. A survey of 1912 listed 8000 cases
of malaria among the employees of Steel and their families
resident either in or around the twenty-two Steel villages.
In the villages alone were 4840 cases. Since tropical
medical experience had definitely identified the mosquito
as the chief carrier of malaria, the first step in fighting
the disease was to rid the neighborhood of mosquitoes.
As a result the incidence of malaria in the T. C. & I.
villages dropped by more than nine tenths, from 4840 to
370 cases in one year, and at present malaria is one of the
least of that area's public health problems, with only ten
to twenty cases a year.

The medical service set up at the same time established
new standards. Nearly all employees availed themselves
of these services at the low rate of $1.25 per month per

family, which fee entitled all its members to professional treatment at the base hospital at Fairfield, Alabama.

This hospital became the clearing house and centre of the health department's work. Thoroughly modern, it houses 310 patients and, with adjoining structures, accommodates a fixed staff of sixteen physicians, covering the various specialties; ten internes; fourteen graduate nurses; and training schools for both white and Negro nurses to a total in both schools of about seventy. Eight dental clinics are maintained, one at the base hospital and seven at the larger dispensaries. Pediatric clinics for both white and colored children are held in each village, with home visits by nurses and social workers. In an average year more than 200,000 patients were treated at dispensaries and nearly 100,000 calls made at homes of employees. Medical examinations of school children were inaugurated in schools for both white and colored pupils, with a total enrollment above 5000, most of whom had never seen a toothbrush or received regular instruction in personal hygiene.

With facilities and services more or less similar to those in the Alabama district, Steel met the social and family needs of its workers in all the other areas where its plants are located. In the iron country of Minnesota, in the newly opened coal regions of Kentucky and the older coal and coke towns of Pennsylvania, Steel has its towns, hospitals, dispensaries, and the like, as in Alabama, but usually without duplication due to the color line. In the steel towns grouped around Pittsburgh, and in Gary, Indiana, the employees are afforded opportunity, under the provisions of the Corporation's Home Owning Plan, to own their homes upon favorable purchase terms. In many areas it maintains general stores, open to all buyers, which are usually the most attractive in the community in both appearance and prices.

Except where irresponsibility of certain groups of workers makes cash payments inadvisable from the family standpoint, store tickets are issued only upon request; in general, Steel workers are paid in cash and buy where they please. Steel meets local variations from a practical point of view, leaving to local direction the adjusting of its general policy to local needs. Gradually it has been widening the scope of employee participation in the operation of welfare services, especially in the field of recreation. This tremendous programme of human welfare was based upon industrial activity. Its backers looked upon the Steel towns and mining villages as busy places where men would go on creating under able direction enough wealth to provide a margin for recreation, health services, sanitary inspections, schooling, pensions, and all the other burdens.

Through nearly all the years of Judge Gary's long leadership these flourishing conditions obtained. The Corporation prospered, expanded, and added to its surplus; its employees had full-time employment, rising wages, better living. Growing automobile demand for steel more than offset declines in rail orders, steel construction gained steadily, and through several years war demand was urgent. Such slumps as occurred were of short duration, ending in booms marked by rising tonnage. Could this pace be maintained? While the whole country was marching recklessly toward disaster, the new head of Steel, Myron C. Taylor, quietly laid his plans to buttress his corporation as strongly as human foresight could arrange against the misfortunes which he foresaw in the offing as a result of America's mad splurge.

When Mr. Taylor took over the leadership of United States Steel in 1928, not only was the boom in full cry, but also the Corporation was ending an epoch. That the out-

side world did not know. Every great consolidation suc-
ceeds or fails on the strength of its human resources. The
original Steel Corporation was a combination of certain
well-managed, successful units functioning under the men
who had brought them up. The Corporation was not a
unit, but a collection of units, and the great task of Judge
Gary was to keep a number of strong individualists from
working against one another. In this he was aided by that
greatest of all ameliorators — a rising price level.

That epoch really closed several years before Judge
Gary's death. Not only had many of the original operating
men retired, but also the steel business had changed into
something very different from the business that the founders
knew. And the task of the chief executive officer changed
from one primarily of seeing that the companies did not get
into one another's way to one of reorganizing from top to bottom to meet the new needs of changing times. It turned out
that the Corporation also had to be revised to meet that most
difficult of all business situations — a declining price level.

The task of reorganizing is a very different one from
organizing. It involves not only careful analysis but also a
planning of both the human and the material elements.
The planning of the material elements is not particularly
difficult, for the problems resolve themselves into weighing
the engineering facts in the scales of financial ability.
Planning of the human element is a different matter, or a
slip will undo every engineering improvement.

Mr. Taylor was fitted for his post because, in addition
to a matured ability to weigh the material components of
a business structure, he has the patience and the finesse
to carry through the vast human engineering. And his
has probably been the most difficult executive problem
ever undertaken, for on top of the already complex problem

came the depression, with its smashing of dollar values and relations.

Mr. Taylor entered the steel business after a substantial experience as a corporation lawyer, with a large background of financial and industrial experience and a wide range of personal interests, including art, music, education, and charitable activities. His interest in public affairs has been largely confined to intelligent observation and an occasional reticent but penetrating statement. By instinct he seeks to avoid the limelight, although complete avoidance is impossible for the head of so large a business in an America where big business is also big news. He guides, with a deep sense of values and a keen concern for corporate ethics and personnel feelings, the mighty organization confided to his care. Entering into his high responsibility reluctantly, he brought to his post a conservatism which led him to view Steel's position, after the most painstaking analysis supported by a sound and farseeing judgment, not as one capable of infinite expansion, but as one in which the fruits of past progress required maturing.

It is significant that Mr. Taylor's first important move in Steel's reorganization had to do with the corporate structure and culminated in the forepart of 1929 with the redemption of more than $300,000,000 worth of bonds and a resulting reduction of Steel's fixed charges by some $30,000,000 a year. Thus the conservative management of Steel had in fair weather prepared for foul and girded itself for a long pull of adversity. Except for this farsighted action, it is doubtful if Steel could have maintained its existing welfare services through the hours of their greatest need and at the same time have spent millions for the relief of out-of-work employees while the Corporation itself was running large deficits.

Before Mr. Taylor began to cast up critically the possibility of a major letdown in industrial activity, no one in corporate management anywhere had envisioned a situation in which for a long period work and wages would be scarce, deficits chronic, and large numbers of employees and their families without earned income. This unforeseen situation began to emerge when the depression cut steel tonnage in 1929. By the time bottom was touched in 1933, the welfare framework of the Steel Corporation had taken on an immense burden of emergency relief expenditures in answer to its leader's determination that no steel worker or his dependents should lack the essentials of life.

This decision to assist employees until times improved was not an easy one to make. As we all know, it is difficult to keep perspective when we are hard up and to go on spending without prospect of immediate return, in the hope that better times are coming by and by. Corporations find this course even harder to follow than individuals, for they have to weigh all their acts in the light of their responsibilities to stockholders. In such circumstances the first and entirely natural reaction is to trim sail by cutting off corporate activities not directly productive of revenue. If Mr. Taylor had followed that course in the case of Steel, he would have shut off the whole welfare stream; but instead he continued the stream while changing its course somewhat to meet lack of orders and shortage of jobs. His conservatism was big enough to include the conserving of human values and home circles.

As in many other large industries the first readjustment to the new social strains was work-sharing. Hours of work were reduced in an effort to keep every employee in possession of at least some earning power. But as orders continued to decline, individual earnings in some cases fell

Pouring steel into 32,000-pound ingot moulds. After cooling, the moulds are stripped from the ingots, which are then taken to the soaking pits preparatory to rolling

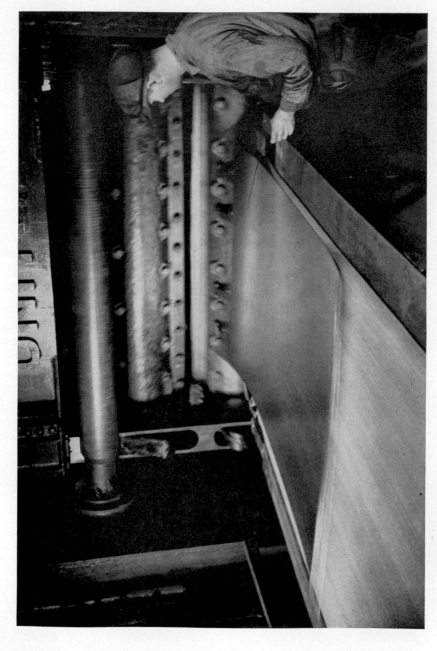

The flying shear which cuts the steel as it uncoils to an accuracy of .125 inch in 10 feet, and at the rate of 400 feet per minute

below family necessities. Those in distress might be living in company-owned houses or in houses which they had purchased on installment. In either case there were no dispossessions, and every effort was made to see that the Steel family had shelter. It was also sure of medical service. Such wages as part-time workers earned were therefore available for food and clothing.

Work fell off more and more until the limits of efficiency were reached for work-sharing. After all, steel-making is a continuous process and as such the shifting of employees has limitations and disadvantages. Lay-offs increased; at the worst point, when steel production was only 10 per cent of the 1929 peak, thousands of employees were entirely without work. Steel provided for them. It met their family needs on food and clothing. It was able to do this gracefully without humiliating the individual because of two existing factors — the company-owned store, with its full stocks of general merchandise; and the knowledge already gained by its social workers of the family problems among the employees. Out-of-work employees were given orders against which the store would deliver merchandise, the entries standing against the individual employee. In districts where stores are not operated, similar arrangements were made through local merchants, the company assuming the obligation and extending credit to the employees. For this purpose the Corporation advanced large sums to its out-of-work employees. Many of these advances were on open account, without interest, security, or evidence of note. This was in addition to direct relief extended for the same purposes. No administrative costs reduced this relief, for the work was all done by employees on company payrolls. Throughout these five difficult years the Steel Corporation has expended annually an average of $15,000,000 for relief, welfare, and pension purposes.

It will get part of this sum back. Hardly had the men returned to work when, little by little, they began to pay off their book accounts at the stores. However, the importance of the effort rests not in the figures involved, although they are large, but in the promptness and informality with which the situation was met. There is an old saying worth repeating in these days of bureaucratic "run-around": "He who gives promptly gives twice." Also let it be remembered that expenditures for both welfare and relief came from a treasury whose reports were showing large deficits from operations. Money for workers' benefits could be found when money for dividends could not be found. Workers and their families were fed, housed, clothed, and nursed out of surplus, a surplus which had been built up in good times and protected by farsighted action in reducing fixed charges. Strictly speaking, the first responsibility of management is to stockholders; in this case management made maintenance of workers a first responsibility.

In meeting the challenge of the depression as it affected employee sustenance, Steel once more stepped out in advance of legislation, just as it did in other respects here briefly summarized : —

1. The Corporation's activities relating to safety, sanitation, and welfare preceded by some time the laws, in many of the states in which its subsidiaries operate, touching these affairs, and no laws anywhere have been adopted setting standards as high as those of the Corporation.

2. The Corporation's provisions for financially caring for injured employees preceded all Workmen's Compensation laws; in fact, those first enacted were based, to a certain extent at least, on the Corporation's voluntary accident relief plan.

3. The housing, sanitary, and general civic standards adopted and put into practice in Corporation towns are above those set by law.

4. Its pension system has been in force many years, and provides annuities for superannuated employees and those who become permanently disabled. No contributions of any kind are made by employees toward the support of this pension plan.

5. The encouraging of home gardens, with instructions in cultivating, as well as instructions in canning, was under way years before the subsistence thought came into general relief.

6. Spreading of whatever work is available at any given time as a matter of relief was inaugurated at the beginning of the depression.

As the depression recedes, its lessons will fade unless they are emphasized now before the details pass from our common consciousness. One of these lessons is that many employers of labor have willingly taken upon themselves responsibilities for employee welfare far beyond the line of duty. In doing so, they kept the worst shocks of adversity from reaching their employees, and in some cases they managed relief so competently and cheerfully that government relief seems cold and sluggish by comparison. Certainly the depression would have been far worse in the cities and villages where Steel operates if management had been unprepared in funds, organization, or humane consideration.

In remarks to stockholders and in other public statements, Mr. Taylor has described the aims, efforts, and responsibilities of the Corporation in dealing with problems incident to the depression. These excerpts illustrate the spirit which dominates its actions: —

The management of the Corporation is burdened with a threefold responsibility to its stockholders, its employees, and the general public. In maintaining a balance between these groups and in order to deal justly with all concerned, it has systematically and methodically taken successive steps to resist the decline in business and earnings by carefully conceived readjustments effected in a manner calculated to occasion a minimum of distress and dislocation in each of these groups. . . .

It has been the constant aim of the directors and executives of the Corporation to so conduct its affairs that it might withstand successfully not only the immediate shocks and difficulties which might arise to perplex it, but also to hold the Corporation, its properties, and associations in such position as to ensure its security, and to enable it to withstand with credit and honor whatever else might be in store for it in the future. To this task all concerned have contributed their utmost in effort, thoughtfulness, and coöperation, and a fine spirit of charity. . . .

No better example of coöperative effort can be found anywhere than that which has been set by the men and women of the United States Steel Corporation since this depression began, and it is safe to say there is no brighter page to be found in industrial history than that which the Steel Corporation wrote through this depression in its treatment of its employees.

AN INDUSTRIAL REPUBLIC

*The Goodyear Programme for Employee
Representation and Education*

III

AN INDUSTRIAL REPUBLIC

IN a democratic society, politics and economics are indissolubly wedded; but, like some other marriages, theirs may be described as one of antagonistic coöperation. As wealth increases through improved business, the twain bicker as they never did when they were poor and their families small. It is rare indeed to find a responsible employer following political precedents and the example of the Federal Government in establishing ways and means of collective bargaining and employee control of important industrial functions.

Yet since 1919 — fifteen years without a strike or serious labor dispute — Goodyear Tire & Rubber Company, America's largest producer in its field, has been functioning comfortably under a representative plan for worker participation in management which is modeled directly upon the Constitution of the United States.

Goodyear's unique system of labor relations, controls, and awards has a deep background. Thirty-five years ago a young engineer from New England — Paul W. Litchfield — brought to Goodyear those strong New England characteristics: technical ability of a high order, a passion for improving goods, and a conviction that ordinary men develop rapidly under the twin stimuli of education and responsibility. Rapidly he changed production methods from those of a "rule-of-thumb" industry, in which foremen without technical education carried their precious "secret" formulas in their vest pockets, to a degree of systematized efficiency which as early as 1916 gave his company first call in the expanding market for automobile tires.

Using a plant newspaper as an avenue of communication between management and labor, he began a steady drive to create in Goodyear a picked body of superior employees. At first, when the factory was small, he could choose employees after personal interviews; but as the factory grew this became impossible. Akron's growing pains added to the difficulties of selection. The town was full of "floaters"; there were two jobs for every man, and only half a house for his family. Labor turnover in the rubber industry, always high, rose to fantastic levels. The time-honored system of leaving the hiring and firing to foremen, who might be acting on whim or grudge toward new employees in the rush for production, seemed to be blocking the superintendent's desire to build a stable working force. Wages, being about double the Ohio average, were a minor cause of grievances; but the dependability and concord essential to a company out to meet automotive demand could not be achieved because of employee-foreman friction. Largely to correct the effects of rapid expansion and occasional hasty decisions, a Labor and Personnel department was created at Goodyear in 1910. This was the first step in creating the broad and strong machinery of negotiation and counsel which is to-day settled Goodyear procedure.

Fruits of this effort appeared when I. W. W. made Akron fighting territory in February 1913. The strike, initiated by some sixty outside organizers, began in another rubber plant, and flared quickly into violence over the whole city, to subside almost as quickly when a force of 1000 citizen vigilantes, assembled after the governor denied troops, took command of the streets under the sheriff's declaration of martial law.

PAUL W. LITCHFIELD
President, Goodyear Tire & Rubber Company

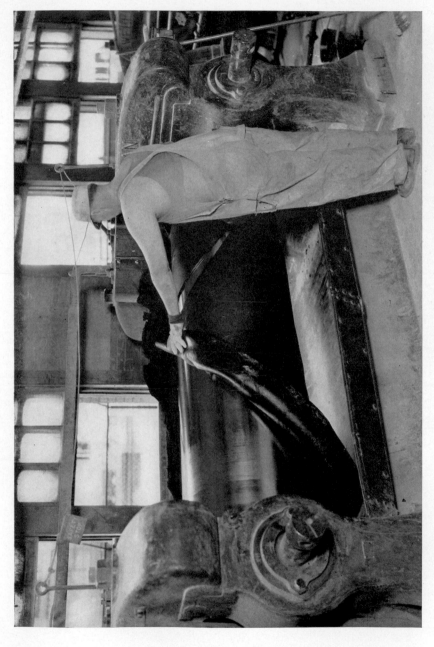

Milling rubber. The grinding action of these rolls thoroughly breaks down the elastic crude rubber and mixes it with other ingredients, such as sulphur

Immediately Goodyear tendered the olive branch to its employees in these words : —

It should be a matter of satisfaction to every Goodyear man that the company came through the strike trouble with a larger percentage of its men loyal, and a larger production, than any other factory affected. Now that the storm is passed, our policy shall be as follows : —

We shall first organize the factory with the force that has remained loyal, and then add to it the men who have gone out because of fear of violence or a difference of opinion. We believe in "one big union" in which all have an interest whether it is those who furnish the labor or those who furnish the capital.

This union stands first of all for a square deal to all, and any differences which may arise will be better settled among themselves than by outsiders who do not understand our conditions. Always bear in mind that the company wants only loyal workmen, and it cannot expect to get them unless it makes its wage scales and working conditions such that people work here because they are better off than they would be anywhere else.

This appeared in the March 1 issue of the factory paper, *Wingfoot Clan*. The name is psychologically pat. Here was a declaration of intent to set up a working clan actuated by an immediate, local loyalty and based upon considerations of mutual defense, the company defending its productivity against interruption and pledging itself to defend its employees by providing better-than-average wages and working conditions. By going almost immediately on the eight-hour day, Goodyear gave proof of intent to carry out its declaration. Within the coming years this industrial clanship would adapt modern conditions to many of the ideals of the olden clans in primitive society, among which were care in choosing members, giving preference to sons of members, heeding seniority and the superior claims of long service, taking care of members in old age, and carrying on through education a tradition of clan prowess. The clan idea in industry, at Goodyear and elsewhere, is one of the irrepressible inside trends in American industry, quietly going forward year after year in many places among great bodies of men, and its social significance is greater than most of us imagine. In the case of Goodyear, I saw its early stages at close hand while managing editor of an Akron newspaper in the year following the great strike, when Goodyear was picking its workmen for the long pull and maturing plans for its successful drive toward first place in tire and rubber manufacture.

The strike had shown the danger of too extreme specialization, since the disaffection of one man might throw many others out of work. A like unbalancing of operations might occur for a variety of other reasons. Consequently Goodyear undertook to train fifty of its best workmen as a Flying Squadron in all branches of manufacture until they became universally proficient, promising to each steady work, a broad education, and higher positions for those who demonstrated marked ability. Since 1913, 1200 men have completed the Flying Squadron training. As a result no industrial emergency finds Goodyear unprepared in trained man-power. When the World War drove Goodyear into rapid expansion in Akron and in other areas, 350 master rubber workers with Squadron training were available to start the new enterprises. As Goodyear became a worldwide business, establishing tire factories in Canada, California, Alabama, England, Australia, Java, and Argentina, cotton operations in the South and New England, and plantation activities in Sumatra, the Squadron provided the shock troops around whom the new activities could be efficiently organized. For instance, 107 Squadron men went to the California plant near Los Angeles, 29 to Gadsden, Alabama, 41 to the English operation at Wolverhampton, 29 to South America, and 12 to Java, including 2 from Australia.

The interchange of men between the home plant and the foreign operations is still active, a tour of foreign duty being esteemed an educational opportunity for men in line for home advancement after recall. Goodyear cultivates the world point of view. Thirteen years after he was assigned, as a stenographer with three years of service, to the leadership of the first Flying Squadron, Cliff Slusser became Vice President and Factory Manager with charge of production in all plants.

The Squadron was a Litchfield idea, part of the educational programme which the general superintendent originated as basic in his plan to give Goodyear superior man-power. Americanization courses for foreign-born workers and training of foremen were other phases of a labor policy in which careful selection, education, and enlarged opportunity for ambitious workers received equal attention. A discerning man cannot talk with Paul W. Litchfield for ten minutes without comprehending that he is an educator no less than a technician and executive. Under his leadership Goodyear has been applying adult education to the making of men and tires.

In 1915, while Mr. Litchfield was still superintendent, he gave $100,000, or one quarter of his fortune, to Goodyear employees, delegating the management of the fund to an association of older workers. From 1915 to 1920, $150,000 in cash was distributed from earnings of this nest egg, a feat made possible by the high earnings of Goodyear stock in which the fund was invested. Since 1930 all its revenues, above regular and special awards, have gone for relief purposes.

The seed sown in 1915 by Goodyear's superintendent in his personal dividend to employees brought forth abundant fruit after the close of the World War, when the Company announced Goodyear Hall as a centre for a broad educational and recreational programme. The Company had enjoyed huge earnings, maintained high dividends in both stock and cash, and this investment was viewed as the equivalent of a stock dividend to labor.

This six-story building, 170 by 400 feet in size, is the focus for all the employee activities of Goodyear in Akron. Here is housed Goodyear Industrial University, the largest corporately supported industrial educational institution in the United States, with a registration of 1322 students in 1932–1933 and attendance of more than 1800. Its broad curriculum may be divided into two parts. The first is general, open to all qualified employees, and organized as follows : —

Preparatory. — For those lacking in such fundamentals as elementary English and elementary arithmetic.

High School Course. — For those who are prepared to round out an interrupted high school education. Credits are accepted by the State of Ohio and diploma entitles holder to enter college on the same basis as public high school graduates.

Institute Course. — The equivalent of junior college instruction, chiefly attended at night by married men. A four-year course, two semesters of 18 weeks each, three hours a week. Subjects especially stressed are economics, accounting, and management.

College Course. — For better-prepared students in engineering and scientific subjects. Three years' work, three hours a week.

Seminars. — One to three hours a week, instruction especially planned for staff and factory employees in supervisory work and otherwise prepared.

College Graduate Training School. — Limited to college graduates and designed to adjust their theoretical knowledge to factory processes and administration. Includes classroom study, shop experience, lectures, and round-table discussions.

As distinct from these general courses, three special courses are given to selected men, as follows : —

1. Flying Squadron, divided between production and engineering. A three-year course, four hours' attendance a week, and geared to Goodyear problems in administration and science.
2. Goodyear Apprentice School, a three-year course for youths between 18 and 21, who divide their time equally between school work and shop work. Sons of Goodyear employees are given preference. More than 350 applicants were interviewed for the 18 places open in this year's "freshman class."
3. Supervisional Training School. This three-year course is open to foremen of all classifications — department foremen, shift foremen, supervisors or subforemen, and certain representatives of staff departments. Of the 800 or 900 men eligible, 200 are usually enrolled for courses in a broad curriculum.

The teaching staff numbers 20 full-time instructors, and a number of part-time instructors.

On April 15, 1935, was celebrated the twentieth anniversary of industrial education at Goodyear. This practical plan of fitting the individual for enlarged opportunities in industry and for better citizenship has been studied by many educators, and some of its lessons have been incorporated into public educational systems.

The Goodyear Hall educational programme began to function coincidentally with the Goodyear Industrial Assembly, certainly the most comprehensive employee representation plan matured by any American company, and, as far as I know, the most successful over a long period of years. That it has not been more generally followed is unfortunate but understandable, because the Goodyear plan involves long preparation in advance, endless patience, and more expense than the simpler and more popular plans for organizing what are commonly called company unions.

The philosophy underlying Goodyear's rather elaborate system of employee relations can be found in a booklet by its idea-father, P. W. Litchfield, published in 1919 under the significant title of *The Industrial Republic*. After stating his opinion that a political democracy and industrial autocracy cannot long endure in the same society, he presents a case for industrial democracy founded upon labor citizenship developing under growing responsibilities toward complete management : —

The time has now arrived when encouragement must be given to the progressive evolution of industry from the state where labor hires itself out to capital, to the state where labor will manage the business and undertake the obligations which are necessary to insure those who have capital that they may safely lend it to the Organization of those who labor, for the mutual benefit of both.

Steps in that direction, as indicated by the author, are the ferreting out of injustice, the education of labor, and the establishing of confidence between labor and management. He said: "Too much has been spent in the past to obtain the good will of the customer and of those who furnish the capital, and too little to obtain the good will of labor."

Goodyear had long outgrown the simple labor relations of small business based upon personal contacts of management and men. Since 1910 the Labor department had lifted the quality of Goodyear workmen through careful selection and training. The foundation having been laid for effective labor representation in management, Mr. Litchfield stood ready to introduce the political methods of democracy into Goodyear's labor relations, in the faith that a superior labor force would make fair use of its new powers.

In searching for a model, he could find none more suitable than the bicameral representative plan embodied in the Constitution of the United States, with its Senate and House of Representatives elected by citizens on an equal suffrage basis. A Council of Industrial Relations composed of executives, elected foremen, and wage earners debated his basic idea, and wrote a Constitution which was ratified by vote of the factory force. It provided for a Senate of 20 members and a House of 40 members, none of them foremen, elected by secret ballot, with right to legislate on all matters pertaining to working conditions, including wages, subject to veto by the factory manager.

The two houses function almost precisely as their prototypes in Congress, through committee reports, parliamentary procedure, and, in case of disagreement, conference between the two bodies. After four years of increasing detail it was decided that minor matters could be disposed of more quickly by a standing joint committee system. A standing joint conference of 24 members — 12 each from the Assembly and the management — still further reduced the labors of the Assembly. These bodies were created by amendment, initiated by the Assembly and ratified by the employees as a common-sense means of speeding up the settlement of grievances, and their decisions are subject to Assembly review.

Company officers may attend Assembly meetings, but speak only upon request, being otherwise barred from the floor. The Assembly receives copies of official reports and informal interim reports. For many years, upon invitation, President Litchfield has made reports to the Assembly similar to those made to the Board of Directors. In both gatherings he finds almost identical reactions, almost the same questions asked, and the same ready acceptance of frank explanations.

Interest taken by rank-and-file workers in Assembly elections runs high. Anyone on the payroll can vote, and the 1934 election brought 86.1 per cent of the eligible voters to the polls. Half of the old Assembly members were reëlected, a higher percentage than usual, which is a fair test of employee satisfaction during a period of more than usual tension in the industrial world at large. From the beginning the Assembly has stimulated literacy, command of English, and acquaintance with parliamentary procedure.

To management the 60 elected Assemblymen are Goodyear labor, truly representative of a body too large for effective expression otherwise. As such it exercises a general control of all employee relationships and activities. The Assembly and its correlated bodies in 1934, a sample year, acted in the following matters: —

Regulated layoffs by extending the seniority rule

Simplified certain wage rates held to be too complicated and negotiated a 10 per cent increase in wages for all employees

Collected data on the cost of living in Akron and, using these as a yardstick, revised rates for idle time

Bettered working conditions by recommendations as to lighting, ventilation, safety devices, and sanitary devices

Arranged special employees' sales for household necessities

Impregnating fabric with rubber on a calender at the Akron factory of the Goodyear Tire & Rubber Company

Tire construction by the flat or band-built method. Built up ply by ply, the tire is later formed by the insertion of an air bag before moulding

Improved transportation service

Administered various relief funds by passing on special cases and
awards

Consolidated the Goodyear Hospital Association with the previously formed Relief Association, forming a bloc of 16,000
Akron residents whose sick expenses are guaranteed

Under the Goodyear system the Assembly as a whole
considers individual grievances only when all other efforts
to bring harmony have failed, but Assemblymen represent
workers in their sections in adjusting personal and group
grievances with supervisors and foremen and act on sectional
joint committees, ten in number.

Through its fifteen years of operation Goodyear Industrial
Assembly has been modified by amendment to avoid delays
incidental to full parliamentary procedure, and to bring
detail grievances to the attention of conferees close to the
situation involved in order to effect prompt settlement.
In this way labor and management have become schooled
to the give-and-take of calm collective bargaining. On
the management side the active conferees are usually men
who entered Goodyear young and have never known any
other attitude toward or method of adjusting disputes.
On the labor side, the majority of elected representatives
are usually either men of long service likewise habituated
to conference methods or young men who have passed
through a training somewhat similar to that of the conferees
on the other side of the table. Labor representatives know
as much about the Company's position as the leading
executives do and in many cases more than the minor
executives do, a situation which led directly to the supervisional training course.

Goodyear Industrial University and Goodyear Industrial
Assembly condition the whole effort in this largest of rubber

and tire companies. As a result, activities which elsewhere would be notable are with Goodyear merely long established routine, under Assembly control or review. Among these are : —

Vacations on pay for all employees with five years or more of service to their credit. Last year the Company gave paid vacations to 10,000 employees.

Thirty-five per cent of all Goodyear employees, including all Goodyear University students, enter into some form of athletic or gymnastic training. Intramural leagues, based on departments, play regular schedules in softball, basketball, tennis, handball, bowling, ping-pong, and swimming contests. A gymnasium, playing fields, and Wingfoot Lake resort are open to all employees.

Goodyear Employees Activities Committee supervises the programmes and manages the funds of more than twenty social clubs, which use Goodyear Hall and allied facilities.

Immediately after passing the physical examination on being employed, Goodyear employees become eligible to the Employees Relief Association, which for 90 cents a month provides personal medical service, hospitalization, and cash benefits while the worker is laid up. Industrial accidents are, of course, covered by compensation insurance law, and the fatality of death by group insurance — the three insurance projects taken together giving every employee coverage against the major risks of life. The Company has $23,000,000 worth of insurance in effect to protect employees.

Since 1916 Goodyear has had a pension system under which a man 65 years of age who has had more than 15 years of service may retire on a pension proportionate to his total earnings in service. A fund for this purpose was set up, and to it has been added one per cent of each year's payroll, accretions bringing the fund up to $2,900,000 at present. The Industrial Assembly recommended adding an employee contributory feature to the

Pension Fund, but this was laid on the table pending possible Federal legislation. The fact that Goodyear is still a young organization is proved by the presence of only 91 men on the pension rolls.

The Goodyear setup in employee relations is unique in American industry, and thus far has escaped serious challenge by outside labor organizations, even in times of extreme industrial discontent. If the proof of the pudding is in the eating, one can say that the Goodyear plan has succeeded.

In the opinion of its originator, President Litchfield, the Goodyear labor philosophy will succeed in any industrial undertaking where it can be founded upon the essentials of consistently high wages, an intelligent labor staff, and a management determined upon fairness. Adapted to local conditions, Goodyear's labor philosophy and methods have been transferred undamaged to cotton mills in the South and in New England, to tire factories in Alabama and Los Angeles, and to foreign factories. Portuguese workers in New Bedford fell into line as heartily as the men of Akron. In England and Australia, both highly unionized lands, no opposition was encountered after labor officials had seen Goodyear policies in action. Justice being a universal human desire, Goodyear finds its American brand acceptable elsewhere. No strike has occurred in the Akron plant since this comprehensive employee relations plan went into effect fifteen years ago.

One final point. What do the workmen at Goodyear get out of this in dollars and cents? Are the various advantages in industrial relations in reality given to employees in lieu of wages? Are they in effect paid for by the employees with money which otherwise would have gone into the pay envelope?

It is commonly charged that the so-called "company unions" cannot bargain as effectively as can an outside group subject to dismissal. This is a pragmatic world. After all, what has been actually accomplished under the Industrial Assembly plan in the vital matter of wages?

In the first place, there seems to be little bargaining at Goodyear in the ordinary sense, collective or otherwise. Bargaining implies two persons, each suspicious of the other, each trying to get as much as he can, conceding as little as he must. There is little or none of that hostile bargaining spirit around Goodyear.

Much detail Assembly work is done by regional committees, each composed of six Assemblymen, six men from the management, and others in the department who have worked together, know each other, and are familiar with conditions. It is almost impossible to be hasty or arbitrary when you are sitting across the table from a man who knows the circumstances as well as you do. There are two sides to most stories, and in the battledore and shuttlecock of committee sessions all present understand that Goodyear stands generally committed to a fair deal and a wage level as good as or a little better than the going rate. When all the facts are assembled, by men close to the dispute, the issue usually resolves itself. In a very large number of cases the vote is unanimous.

Still, the recorded results of wage agreements since 1919 are impressive as showing the advance of a large labor body in purchasing power. After the 1920–1921 depression, the Assembly raised the question of a 10 per cent wage increase in April 1922, and won it, Goodyear being one of the first companies to raise wages after that depression. During the prosperous years following, wages rose proportionately to general wages, to fall again in 1930 as the new depression struck. When conditions showed improvement in the spring of 1933, the Assembly asked for a 10 per cent blanket increase in May, received it, received a second raise of 7½ per cent in August and a third of virtually 10 per cent in August 1934, with the result that the average hourly earnings in 1935 are higher than they were in 1929.

October figures from the United States Department of Labor show the average hourly earnings of employees in all industries standing at 55.4 cents an hour. Goodyear employees, male and female, skilled and unskilled, were then earning 88 cents an hour on the average. Certain large skilled groups were earning $1.15 to $1.26.

If President Litchfield were asked to explain how the various employee activities which cost substantial sums can be maintained, along with a liberal wage scale in a period of intensive competition and bedrock manufacturing costs, he would probably tell you that a cheap man is a poor investment at any price. Good men turn out better merchandise, and a liberal wage scale is a continuous and stimulating challenge to every man in management to do an efficient job. Beyond all that, unquestionably there is a distinct cash value to any corporation in any practical method of reducing expensive, and sometimes demoralizing, labor turnover to almost the vanishing point. The Goodyear methods, farsighted and comprehensive as they are, work exceptionally well in the conditions which surround the rubber industry.

THE LAMP OF RESEARCH

General Electric's Great Adventure after Knowledge

IV

THE LAMP OF RESEARCH

"The only perpetual motion is the growth of truth."

One might expect to find this sentence in a sermon by a liberal divine, or in a dog-eared treatise on moral philosophy from those far-off days when generalists, not specialists, prospered. Certainly we should hardly look for its author among the scientists. Yet that epigram is one of many from a man who for thirty-four years has been probing with a group of scientists the mysteries of energy and matter, in behalf of a great industrial company which brings the results into common use as soon as practical. The company is General Electric; the man, Dr. Willis R. Whitney, organizer and for many years head of its Research Laboratory, and to-day vice president in charge of research.

This drive against the unknown goes forward on a wide front and involves every manœuvre known to military science — scouting and reconnaissance; forlorn-hope charges; isolated sieges as this or that objective becomes defined. But always in these lesser engagements the grand plan of advancing all along the line has been held steadfastly in mind by men at once patient and impatient — impatient with human ignorance, patient with the complexities of nature.

The objective is nothing less than solving the riddle of the universe, to reach the fullest understanding of infinite and infinitesimal reactions of matter and energy which swing the stars in their courses and charge powerfully through all animate and inanimate forms, down to the living cell and the eternal dance within the atom of positron and electron. Long before the limits of comprehension have been reached, these forces and their habitats have escaped the narrow limits of human vision; but delicate instruments record their motions and reactions so definitely that their conduct can be examined by human intellect. Fortunately the invisible world functions so dependably that upon the output of its titanic energy man has built a civilization based on improved industrial operations, a network of power-and-light lines reaching out from electric service stations, a system of communication which conquers distance with the speed of light, and a general flexibility of motion applicable to mechanical processes which has routed darkness, eased toil, and increased wealth.

Nevertheless, with all these great advances, electrical research is still a pioneer enterprise on the road to immensities and services as yet undreamed.

When Benjamin Franklin in 1752 risked his life to draw electricity down a kite-flown wire, and with it charged a Leyden jar, he demonstrated that the force which flung long sparks through the heavens was identical with that in short sparks produced by hand on friction machines. Later experimenters knew that even in their laboratories they were dealing with the cosmic. Joseph Henry with his induction coil, Morse with his telegraph, Bell with his first telephonic communication, all must have felt the truth of Morse's message, "What hath God wrought!"

With the practical success of the telegraph, the gates of the Electrical Age swung ajar, but the nation was a full century old before the public gained more than a glimpse of the wonders to come. At the Centennial Exposition at Philadelphia in 1876, two feeble electric dynamos were

GERARD SWOPE
President, General Electric Company

OWEN D. YOUNG
Chairman of the Board, General Electric Company

The world's largest hydroelectric generators, weighing 2,000,000
pounds and 32 feet in height, under construction at Schenectady
for harnessing the mighty power of the Colorado

on display, each connected with a single arc lamp. But these portents of the future were hidden away in corners and overshadowed by the mighty steam engines, which held alike the centre of the stage and the admiration of the public.

The electrical exhibits at the Centennial, however, stirred the inventive mind of America. Within a few years several men who deservedly rate as General Electric pioneers began careers which eventually brought significant inventions of theirs into one institution. In Cleveland, Charles F. Brush improved the dynamo by reducing its internal friction; by 1878 he had made the arc light, in series of sixteen, practicable for sale. In Philadelphia, Elihu Thomson invented the first practical method of electric welding, the first dynamo to produce either direct or alternating current, the first vibrating arc lamp mechanism, and the first automatic regulation of lamps in series. In Brooklyn, James J. Wood constructed his closed-coil dynamo, capable of operating at 10,000 volts. And at Menlo Park, in 1876, Thomas Edison began those long experiments with the incandescent lamp which were destined to make lighting history and to lift their author into public affection.

So far this story of electricity in America has been one of invention rather than research. The inventor aims at creating or improving a specific product. In his experiments he may encounter unfamiliar effects, as Thomson did in his accidental shifting of brushes, from the results of which he immediately caught and applied the principle of automatic regulation. Sometimes the experiment is so long continued that a considerable body of by-product knowledge is built up, as in Edison's search for the carbon filament. Edison held to the main line; he knew what he was after. Engaged in pure research, he would have felt free to follow any interesting lead as it developed, and by so doing he would have learned more about the fundamental nature of electricity, from which he might have been able to predict that carbon would be a workable filament. At that time, his direct attack may have been the only, or at least the quickest, means of gaining his objective. The carbon lamp was a tremendous advance. But of late years equally great advances in the lamp field have come from information acquired in researches undertaken to expand knowledge rather than to improve product.

Between its organization in 1892 and the end of the century, the General Electric Company, captained by Charles A. Coffin, arrived far ahead of its time at this point of view on research: while there is no limit to the extension of knowledge in electricity, there are definite limits to the imagination of men working to apply an unknown force to mechanisms for public use. Tinkering, no matter how intelligent, can go just so far. Consequently the more we can learn of energy and matter, the more fully we have insured the future.

This opinion probably originated in conversations of E. W. Rice, Jr., vice president and technical director; Charles Proteus Steinmetz, head of the consulting department; A. G. Davis, in charge of the patent department; and Elihu Thomson. At his home Steinmetz maintained a laboratory of his own; but he saw that the future of research belonged not to the lone worker but to the informed and cohesive group of specialists, well equipped and financed, that could follow investigations wherever they led without concessions to immediacy. The Company already had adequate engineering laboratories; what it needed now was a laboratory devoted to scientific research of the broadest type.

To organize the new laboratory Mr. Rice chose Dr. Whitney, then a young professor of chemistry at Massachusetts Institute of Technology, who elected to come to Schenectady in order to be near Steinmetz. These three projected a laboratory unique in American industrial history, one that would have a free hand in pursuing researches in pure science and yet have the financial backing of a great industry. Assured on this point, Dr. Whitney began to gather a staff which upon his retirement as Director, in 1932, numbered more than three hundred. When the stern test of the war came in 1917, the electrical industry was found to be one of the few in which America could claim self-sufficiency and world leadership, thanks in no small part to General Electric and the American Telephone and Telegraph Company, another electrical enterprise that early undertook to finance research in pure science.

The Research Laboratory grew slowly, with rigid selection of personnel. There was no pressure for immediate commercial results, and some years elapsed before the knowledge accumulated through research developed any new products. Then came the new high-resistance electric furnace, productive of high temperatures, which was to help produce the Gem lamp, first large-scale improvement in lamps since Edison's invention of thirty years before. In scientific research one turns up unexpected treasures along the road. Whitney, "playing with" his electric furnace, gradually became convinced that by means of it he could test a theory of his on the cause of the blackening of lamp bulbs, a limiting factor on their life and efficiency. He discovered that carbon filaments, heated to new high temperatures, developed, when placed in lamps, increased electrical resistance as furnace temperatures went up. Whitney's new carbon filaments had been changed by the heat into a form of graphite, which would withstand a higher temperature than the prior carbon filaments. Thus in five years the Research Laboratory arrived at a substantial improvement in incandescent lighting by a route which involved pure research, the invention of an intermediary machine, and its use in a way undreamed of at the time of its invention. The efficiency of electric lighting had been increased 25 per cent, and the lamp of 1905 had double the light output of Edison's early lamps.

In those early days news of laboratory findings filtered through the whole organization by a sort of natural osmosis. But the success of the Gem lamp so thoroughly proved the wisdom of basic research that the research staff began to grow in numbers. Increasing size and multiplicity of crisscross research problems required a closer organization and a more definite liaison between research, engineering, and manufacturing. The research staff now works in sections, each under a leader. Division of work between these groups is, of course, on a functional rather than a topical basis. For instance, research on air conditioning, which involves many factors, is broken down until it receives the attention of several groups — chemistry, dealing with the factors of air content and odors; metallurgy, which handles corrosion; mechanics, dealing with noise, vibrations, air circulation, and kindred problems.

The field of air conditioning affords an excellent example of the interplay of research and engineering in a great industry. The research staff has no direct responsibilities for engineering. Regular reports on progress in research are circulated to engineering departments in all plants; engineers adapt these findings to their production needs, perhaps calling for special reports on moot points. Occasionally the engineers, having gone so far with the knowledge in hand, will ask the research department to conduct further work along a given line in order to surmount a final barrier. For example, the designing of air-conditioning systems brought before the research staff a request for quieter ventilating machinery, which in due course was met.

On occasions the Research Laboratory enters the manufacturing arena, its scientists directing the production of devices of so novel or delicate a character that engineering and manufacturing departments have no precedents under which those innovations could be produced. For instance, when the product was new, members of the research staff were engaged in producing the Coolidge X-ray tube. After correct factory procedure had been demonstrated by the research department, this activity was split off and became a separate manufacturing division, born, reared, and trained by research.

A constant contact is maintained between engineering and research through Dr. W. D. Coolidge, Director, and L. A. Hawkins, Engineer of the Research Laboratory, who call the attention of engineers to research developments and arrange such conferences as are necessary.

Dr. Coolidge came to General Electric in 1905 from a post as assistant professor of physicochemical research at Massachusetts Institute of Technology. In 1908 he became Assistant Director, in 1928 Associate Director, and in 1932 Director. His achievements, too many to be related here in full, include ductile tungsten. Tungsten filaments marked a distinct step forward in the development of the electric lamp, a product touching the pocketbook of the average citizen. Both Edison and Gem lamps had carbon filaments. For thirty years carbon ruled as the accepted filament material, although much research had been devoted to the attempt to find a substitute with better properties.

At last tungsten entered the electrical scene in an Austrian laboratory. This metal, notable for its high melting point and extreme hardness, long defied attempts to work it into wire. The Austrian investigators developed a tungsten filament through a process of squirting threads of a paste containing powdered tungsten, then baking and sintering the threads until the paste and the impurities were vaporized out, leaving pure tungsten particles welded together to form a filament. Though fragile, the new metal filament had the advantage of high luminosity. How could it be made stronger and more enduring?

Years passed before Dr. Coolidge could isolate the causes of gains made more or less at random and bind the chain of causation into a positive technique. At length ductile and tough tungsten for lamp filaments was produced by heating the metal to a point only slightly below fusion, hammering it with a special technique at an elevated temperature, then reheating and repeating the operation at successively lower temperatures until the wire acquired great strength and became ductile when cold. Tungsten could now replace carbon in lamps and double the efficiency of electricity in illumination. The Research Laboratory had decidedly lowered the cost of lighting in 1905; in 1911, with the tungsten lamp, it cut the cost again in half. The householder's dollar bought four times as much light in 1911 as it had in the early days of incandescent lighting.

Dr. Irving Langmuir, Associate Director of the Laboratory, who recently won the Nobel Prize for his researches in chemistry, — being the first American industrial scientist to receive that international award, — took the next step on the way toward perfection in electric lamps. So far all electric lamps, whether carbon or tungsten, were vacuum lamps; the vacuum idea had become fixed. Improving

GENERAL ELECTRIC'S TRIUMVIRATE OF SCIENCE

Left, Dr. Irving Langmuir; centre, Dr. Willis R. Whitney; right, Dr. W. D. Coolidge

(*Painted by H. M. Mott-Smith*)

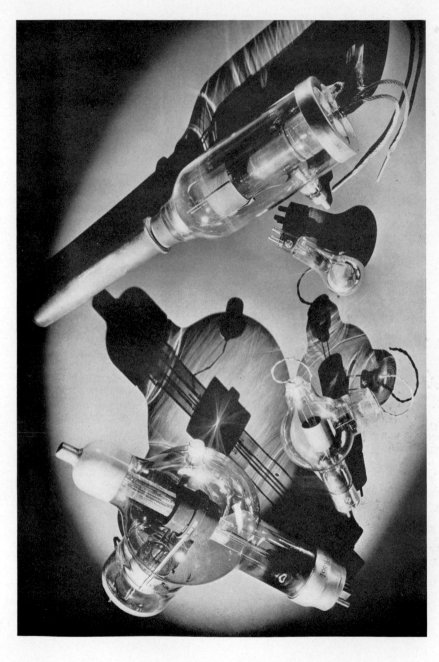

High-voltage vacuum tubes, truly a product of research, are being used more and more in industry for control of processes and mechanical motions

lamps meant either improving the filament or improving the vacuum. Whoever strives for a perfect vacuum is in for a discouraging struggle against Nature; as long as the vacuum remained an essential part of lamp-lighting, its imperfections limited progress. The war against bulb-blackening had to be reopened on another front after tungsten and high temperatures replaced carbon and lower temperatures. Not all tungsten lamps grew black, but enough of them did to present a problem which Dr. Langmuir, coming to the Research Laboratory from the faculty of Stevens Institute in 1909, chose as his first subject of research here.

Dr. Langmuir had recourse to a well-established research method which is akin to homeopathic medicine: *similia similibus curantur*. The thought processes behind this elaborate research are beautifully presented in one of Langmuir's papers, in which he said: —

I really did n't know how to produce a better vacuum, and instead proposed to study the bad effects of gases by putting gases in the lamp. I hoped that in this way I would become so familiar with these effects of gas that I could extrapolate to zero gas pressure, and thus predict, without really trying it, how good the lamp would be if we could produce a perfect vacuum.

This principle of research I have found extremely useful on many occasions. When it is suspected that some useful result is to be obtained by avoiding certain undesired factors, but it is found that these factors are very difficult to avoid, then it is a good plan to increase deliberately each of these factors in turn so as to exaggerate their bad effects, and thus become so familiar with them that one can determine whether it is really worth while avoiding them.

By this method Langmuir discovered not only that perfect vacuum was unnecessary, but also that it was undesirable. When the glass bulb was filled with the inert gases argon and nitrogen in correct quantity, better illumination was secured, especially with large filaments coiled in a close helix. Lamp efficiency shot up more than 100 per cent.

These three major improvements in lighting — Whitney's in 1905, Coolidge's in 1911, and Langmuir's in 1914 — decreased the cost of electrical illumination to one fifth of what it had been at the turn of the century. Encouraged by reduced lamp and current costs, the public bought more electricity. If America were to return to the carbon lamp immediately preceding Whitney's, it would have to pay, on the basis of present use of light, $2,000,000,000 more per year for current, or more than $5,000,000 a night additional. This indicates the public's stake in General Electric research. The annual saving to the American people through advances in lamp efficiency alone, and overlooking the research department's many other contributions, is more than ten times the Company's capitalization.

Langmuir's studies of incandescent filaments in gases led not only to an emphatic increase in lamp efficiency, but also to the development of a radically new type of electric welding, the atomic hydrogen welding arc. In his investigation of the different gases in lamps he found that the heat losses from tungsten filaments in hydrogen at high temperatures did not follow the usual law for gases, as did hydrogen at low temperatures. His researches showed that the incandescent filament broke down the stable molecules of hydrogen gas — each of two atoms — into atomic hydrogen. Dr. Langmuir found that more atomic hydrogen was formed by passing an electric arc between tungsten electrodes in a jet of hydrogen. Blown out of the arc by the gas pressure, the atomic hydrogen recombines to molecular form, with an intensely hot flame and liberating about half again as much heat as does the oxyhydrogen flame.

This principle has been incorporated in the atomic hydrogen welding equipment, which makes it possible to fabricate various metals which previously could not be welded satisfactorily. Alloys containing chromium, aluminum, silicon, or manganese, among others, are usually difficult to weld, since at high temperature these elements are oxidized in air, changing the quality of the alloy. Atomic hydrogen is a powerful reducing agent, preventing the formation of oxides; hence, by use of the atomic hydrogen flame, iron can be melted or welded without contamination by carbon, nitrogen, or oxygen, and, similarly, various alloys and other metals can be handled without fluxes and without oxidation. The atomic hydrogen welding arc — resulting from pure research investigations — has decidedly broadened the field of welding, and has been put to work in many industrial fields.

Radio broadcasting, also, owes much to Langmuir's researches. More than fifty years ago Edison noted and reported a destructive blue glow surrounding the terminals in some of his carbon-filament lamps. This he overcame by improving the vacuum. Upon introducing another electrode he found that a current passed from the heated filament to the electrode, provided his bulb was "gassy"; this phenomenon became known as the "Edison effect." Not, however, until "wireless" made its entrance upon the electrical scene did the Edison effect gain importance. Then Fleming took advantage of what had been discovered by Edison and produced his detector tube, which immediately outmoded other radio detectors. De Forest followed the same principle in his audion, in which he placed a grid electrode which made his tube not only a better detector but also an amplifier. Both Fleming and De Forest tubes were low voltage and "gassy," and varied in operating characteristics. If the voltage was pushed much above thirty volts the tubes would show blue glow and destroy themselves. Such "gassy" tubes were too weak for practical use in broadcast transmission.

When Langmuir began to study radio tubes, the opinion prevailed that these functioned through mysterious reactions of gases on filaments, but investigation led him to question that opinion. Electrons, he decided, collect around the filament and blanket further emissions until they are removed; this discovery is the now famous "Langmuir space-charge effect." He concluded that gas particles broke down this blanket and permitted electrons to travel from the hot cathode to the other electrode. Such tubes, however, inherently could carry only a small amount of current, at low voltage. The way out was to devise a system for removing the electrons from around the cathode as fast as liberated. Langmuir accomplished this by placing the electrodes closer to each other and employing high vacuum and high voltage. Thus he produced the so-called "pure electron discharge" tube. In this way he removed the limitation of thirty volts, and greatly increased the electron flow, or current. The way to radio broadcasting over immense distances, through further development of tubes of this type, was now open.

Dr. Coolidge had long been interested in X-rays, and had already applied his ductile tungsten in making targets for use in X-ray tubes. He saw in Langmuir's pure electron discharge in high vacuum the possibility of creating a radically new type of tube, now universally known as the Coolidge tube. It represented a complete transformation of the X-ray tube from a temperamental, erratic device, requiring experience and judgment in its operation, to a stable, exactly controllable device, which moreover, in its later developments, proved capable of design for much higher output than the prior X-ray tube. The new Coolidge tube permitted X-ray photographs to be made by physicians in less time and with more clarity and safety, and afforded increased therapeutic possibilities. As a result, the Coolidge X-ray tube soon superseded all others in medical use and has found increasing favor in industry for sub-surface examination of materials.

To Dr. Whitney was due the discovery that artificial fever might be induced by high-frequency radio waves, which led to the development of the high-frequency "fever machine," or "inductotherm," as it is now called. This device, in the hands of doctors, is proving to be a powerful weapon in combating some of the worst diseases.

More and more high-voltage vacuum tubes are being used in industry for control of processes and mechanical motions. Of these the best known is the photoelectric tube, or electric eye, highly sensitive to light gradations, which has been greatly improved at Schenectady. Other products which have come to pass through research staff efforts are the magnetite electrode arc lamp, the Tungar rectifier for charging storage batteries, tungsten points for automobile and airplane ignition systems, the Langmuir vacuum pump, thoriated tungsten filaments for vacuum tubes, the calorizing steel process, sheath wire with mineral insulation for heating elements, Langmuir's atomic hydrogen welding process, synthetic resins such as Glyptal, a wide range of improved electric insulating materials, new vapor lamps, and electronic tubes of many types.

High in any just estimate of the research department's work would come the hundreds of thorough and scholarly papers which the members of the staff have contributed to scientific journals. This output of scientific writing adds to the body of knowledge upon which we must rely as the very foundation of industrial and social progress. The value of the Laboratory has been repeatedly recognized by awards from technical societies to scientific leaders of the Laboratory and by degrees from academic institutions.

The Research Laboratory is only one of many laboratories maintained by the General Electric Company. Each major industrial works has its own laboratory specializing on problems relating to its products. From these works laboratories have often come research results of a high order. Moreover, in the General Engineering Laboratory and in the various engineering departments a multiplicity of developments, such as that of the mercury boiler and turbine by W. L. R. Emmet, is constantly in progress.

In five years, from 1925 to 1929 inclusive, General Electric spent $100,000,000 on research and engineering development. This expenditure resulted in profits to the company, of course, but in far greater profits to the public. A conservative estimate is that for every dollar of profit the General Electric Company has made on its innovations the public has been saved from ten dollars to one hundred dollars. Above that, the public enjoys comforts, conveniences, incentives, and improved processes of production which it never had before and could hardly get as quickly in any other way.

This determined attack on the secrets of nature has another advantage when one recalls the high mortality of companies that have neglected the scientific approach to betterments. In this swiftly changing world, research is the price of continued existence for any large industry depending upon marketing complicated goods and services. In an industry founded upon an unknown force, which electricity still largely is and which it may remain to the end of time, the penalty of letting well enough alone would be certain disaster.

One perceives, also, the influence of industrial research in the everlasting race between the cost of living and the standard of living. Over the centuries the latter has been forging ahead. Cost of living, on the basis of brute subsistence and shelter, has moved in relatively narrow limits, but the standard of living has leaped upward until laborers travel in swifter and more comfortable vehicles than the royal chariots of kings, until humble men live in homes more convenient and sanitary than ancient palaces, and in them enjoy comforts beyond the imagination of earlier Americans. There is no way of continuing this social boon except through the intelligent use of natural forces, which means more research and the prompt application of scientific findings to common use.

The shock troops in the army of progress are the men of science. Politics may beat the drums, finance may move the heavy baggage trains, social workers may help the afflicted and physicians mend the wounded; but science wins the ground, and the rest of us march along in its wake to consolidate its gains. The work goes on in many places, in universities and college laboratories as well as in industrial laboratories, the former being distinguished traditionally for pure science, the latter for applied science. In General Electric the twain meet in exceptionally fruitful endeavor with private capital taking the risks, footing the bills, and passing on to the public the lion's share of the gains made in this phase of the growth of truth.

POURING IDEAS INTO TIN CANS

*Continental Can Company Rises through Applying
New Methods to a Standardized Industry*

V

POURING IDEAS INTO TIN CANS

IF one were searching for examples of the old and new to illustrate the swift changes of our common life through the past century, he need not look beyond the oldest business in the world — retail merchandising, and particularly the grocery store, around which revolves community life at its simplest. Fifty years ago the food and general supply store kept its staple goods in wooden barrels, with an overflow stock in a dingy back room. Barrels of molasses, vinegar, sugar, flour, pickles, kerosene, crackers, and vegetables stood about on the floor. Over these would bend a clerk probably wearing a soiled apron, with a ladle or scoop in his hand, presently to return with his order in a paper bag or wooden dish over which he placed a piece of wrapping paper. Almost the only packaged goods on the shelves were flavoring extracts, cans of salmon, meat, and condensed milk, together with a few articles in wooden or paper boxes.

Enter a similar store to-day. No barrels in sight. Even that familiar human type, the cracker-barrel philosopher, has gone. More than half the store's merchandise is on shelf display, packaged to be handed out in the twinkling of an eye. The contents have been protected by a container against most of the insanitary accidents of transportation and handling and against adulteration or substitution by unscrupulous dealers. The container is the key to modern merchandising and the basis of its guarantees. Each year sees more packaged goods consumed and more sorts of goods vended in containers and steady progress made toward improvement of both the package and its contents, a trend certain to continue because the public finds in it increasing satisfaction, confidence, and convenience. Try to think of any article which, once packaged, has been returned to bulk handling. In thousands of instances the public has voted with its nickels and dimes for container merchandising.

If an observer could step from the 1880's to the present, he would be struck by the presence in amazing variety and quantity of an object now so common that it is taken for granted — the tin can. The few packaged products found in the old-time stores were for the most part in bottles, cartons, and boxes. Now the tin can dominates the food trade, appears decisively in many other lines, including paints, varnishes, pharmaceuticals, cosmetics, polishes, and so forth, and is being adapted to use on more and more products of common sale. Our old-timer, transplanted from one era to another, would fall to wondering how such quantities of tin cans were made, and especially how they could be manufactured with such unvarying success that perfect protection of their contents could be guaranteed.

The spick-and-span store of the present is possible only because in spick-and-span factories, spaced widely over the country, tin cans are being turned out with almost lightning rapidity from tin plate, which consists of a thin sheet of steel coated with pure tin. The cleanest metal-working operation known to an industrial age must surely be that of a can factory. Let us visit one of Continental's modern can plants. A door is opened and the visitor steps through into a sunny room, the air of which seems full of blinding beauty and deafening clatter. Thousands of brightly shining, eloquently tinkling tin cans chase each other through automatic machines and along overhead conveyor systems. Each contributes its small voice to the rattling clamor;

each adds its glinting surface to a kaleidoscopic motion picture. The frame of the pattern holds steady, the lines march unbroken alow and aloft, but each scintillating little soldier dances and sings as it moves, step by tiny step, through this amazing factory.

It is a scene to delight a modernist painter, alert for new combinations of light and shade in flashing motion. Not soon to be forgotten is the orderly beauty of simple, every-day objects, multitudinously on the march and singing as they travel automatically toward their utilitarian destiny. No hand touches them after they pass from slitting machine to storehouse; in fact, no hand has touched the inside of one of them since the tin plate sheets, two tons to a bundle, left the mills.

Comparatively few persons supervise the automatized operation of this plant. This must be "the can maker's paradise." On each of fifteen lines 325 cans may be made every minute of the working day, with 7,000,000 a day a mathematical possibility under continuous operation. Some of Continental's thirty-two can-making plants are larger than this one in volume, some smaller, but all reveal a high efficiency combined with speed. Celerity is the word which from first to last characterizes can making.

In a specialized plant like this one a high degree of auto-matization is attained. The cans are cut, shaped, soldered, sealed on one end, and tested under pressure by machinery more sensitive to flaws than human eye or hand. The last of the hand processes to yield to machinery was soldering. An expert task in craftsmanship was this one of soldering the outside of the seam of an open cylinder as it swung in front of the operator; occasionally one sees this skilled hand operation in a "general-line" plant, when a wide variety of orders, some of which are too small in quantity to justify the high initial cost of extreme automatization, has to be filled. Whereas a specialized plant may make only one or two shapes, the general-line plant often has a hundred shapes and sizes in process at once, ranging from 110-pound coffee drums and 50-pound lard cans to tiny sample containers.

Greatest volume is reached in manufacturing cans for packers of foodstuffs, greatest variety in general-line cans for other goods. Continental's thirty-two can plants may be classified as follows: twelve packers' can plants; fifteen general-line plants; and five combination plants.

The can opener in the kitchen is still the foundation of the business in spite of growth in other lines. Packers' cans are made in or near railroad centres from which transportation lines radiate to important food-growing areas. Both for canners and for can makers, even slight freight-rate advantages are important; as a result, the industrial map of canning operations and can making is dictated largely by the geography and timing of plant growth. Food packing and can making tend toward locations near the growing or producing areas suitable for quantity packs. The largest of these packs consists of evaporated and condensed milk; pineapples, pears, peaches, apricots, cherries, and grapefruit among the fruits; corn, peas, tomatoes, and beans in the vegetable world; soups in all varieties; and salmon, the most popular product of our fisheries. The average reader may be surprised to learn that although Maine, the original corn-canning state, still holds a proud place, the large-volume packs come from Iowa, Indiana, Ohio, Maryland, Minnesota, and Illinois; that California's peaches, better eating after canning than before, are used almost exclusively for commercial canning — very limited quantities of the celebrated Michigan and Georgia peaches being available in the package-goods market; that the largest quantities of tomatoes come from widely separated areas — California, Missouri, Arkansas, Indiana, Ohio, Kentucky, Tennessee, and the Atlantic seaboard area of southern New Jersey and the Delaware peninsula, composed of Delaware and the eastern portions of Maryland and Virginia. Wisconsin and New York are the largest producers of peas for canning.

This picture changes with weather and climate variations, discovery of new insecticides, development of fertilizers, opening of new lands to packable crops, improvement of seeds, and acceptance by growers of changes from traditional to scientific methods of agriculture. In the canning industry the plants are usually located in the small villages or towns close to a favored crop area. The can maker tends to follow the packer, spacing factories widely instead of concentrating operations. Both are answering the call of the land and the dictation of seasonal swings beyond the control of man.

Neither the canner nor the can maker, however, accepts Nature fully or blindly. The former stirs his contract farmers to improve yields in quantity and quality. His agricultural experts advise farmers and market gardeners on crop rotation, tillage, drainage, spraying, and seed selection. Many canners grow and distribute seed to growers, conduct long-range experiments in plant variations, inspect fields of ripening crops, and fix the day and hour when the crop should be gathered to ensure first quality. The old belief that only cull crops go into cans has become a myth; the fact is that the yields of the best acres go with the least possible delay to the plant and into tin cans. It could hardly be otherwise, with processors guaranteeing their products and profits depending on high-speed, continuous runs through short periods, conditions that make the best product infallibly the cheapest.

Another element reënforcing geographical spread is the stark need for prompt, almost instant, service. The food packer cannot wait; it is now or never with him. If his delivered crop exceeds his estimates, he must get containers by rush order. His commercial life hangs on the outcome of his shout for cans. In the case of general-line plants the need for supplies on the instant is not so acute. Nevertheless, canners want containers when they want them — *pronto* and no fooling! As a result, Continental Can Company, Inc., has packers' can plants in ten states, general-line plants in ten states, and combination plants in four states.

Organized with the modest capital of $500,000 in the fall of 1904, Continental acquired the patents and good will of United Machinery Company of Rochester, New York, which had developed a line of improved can-making machinery. With these machines it equipped plants at Syracuse and Chicago, natural centres for can manufacturing because at these points radiating railways tap rich agricultural sections. Shortly thereafter the Company established its third plant at Baltimore. In 1909, seeking assured supply of raw materials, the Company bought the Standard Tinplate Company at Canonsburg, Pennsylvania. In these five years occurred a technical change of great importance, the shift from the soldered end to the sanitary or doubleseamed end now in general use. Under the leadership of its founder and first President, T. G. Cranwell, Continental quickly reëquipped its plants to meet the new situation. Later growth to present proportions has been partly through internal expansion and partly through merger.

Thus far Continental operations had been confined to packers' cans, a highly seasonal business with acute demand from April to October, followed by a comparatively slack season of almost six months. General-line business, on the

OSCAR C. HUFFMAN
President, Continental Can Company, Inc.

Intricate and highly automatic machines test the hermetic properties of each container manufactured

other hand, is steadier; and corporate stability could hardly be gained without it. So Continental entered the general-line field in 1912 at Chicago.

In 1917, with canned goods in demand by the army, there arose the plant at Clearing, Illinois, near Chicago, now the Company's largest operation. Another development of that year was doubling the factory facilities at Syracuse, New York, for the manufacture of can-making and can-closing machinery, the latter designed for installation in packing plants for closing the cans after filling. This meant that Continental could offer its customers machines progressively adapted to every improvement in can design and built to meet particular needs. It became possible to increase the guarantee ratio, now surprisingly high. Continental guarantees 998 out of every 1000 packers' cans it delivers to fruit and vegetable canners.

The war induced a marked change in the food habits of the people, the net effect of which benefited the canning industry. After hostilities ceased, the letdown in this industry was less marked than in some others. The public had become educated to the use and convenience of canned foods, with the result that, with the return of peace, these foods continued in popular favor.

The activities of the twenties reflect particularly the energy and foresight of Carle C. Conway, a Vice President since 1913, who became First Vice President in 1923 and President in December 1926. A piano manufacturer by prior experience, Mr. Conway had long been interested in Continental as a large stockholder. When he became the Continental leader, his vision and driving force soon made themselves felt in vigorous growth. Details of can making and can selling were left to two veterans who had long been in the Company's service, Messrs. F. A. Prahl and S. J.

Steele, Vice Presidents in charge respectively of manufacturing and sales, while Mr. Conway concentrated on enlarging both his company and the markets served by it.

Other officials added to the organization in this period included J. B. Jeffress, Jr., in 1923, as Secretary and Treasurer; J. F. Hartlieb, in 1927 (now Vice President in charge of budgets, credits, and Chairman of the Finance Committee); and I. W. England, in 1928, as a Vice President (now in charge of advertising). Long tenures in office are the rule with this company.

A new general-line plant was built in Jersey City in 1920. In 1926, operations began on the Pacific Coast, which have now reached large proportions. The first Coast plant, acquired at Los Angeles, was expanded two years later. Early in 1927 the Company began can manufacturing at Seattle, where, in addition to the usual output, a special process is used to meet the needs of the Alaska salmon packers. Flattened can cylinders, open at each end, are made at Seattle, shipped to Alaska, and there re-formed into cylinders, bottomed, filled, and sealed — an interesting adaptation of means to an end called forth by transportation costs limiting bulk cargoes in Alaskan trade.

The big year in Continental growth — 1928 — saw expansion in many directions, the most important being the absorption of the United States Can Company, a move which introduced into the Continental organization Mr. O. C. Huffman, President of the Company since 1930 in succession to Mr. Conway, who then became Chairman of the Board. Mr. Huffman had manufactured cans since 1903, when he organized the Virginia Can Company at Buchanan, Virginia, selling most of the stock to farmers. The youthful founder received $100 a month salary and had to fight with his farmer stockholders for that. Virginia's original stock ultimately became a valuable investment for those who clung to it over a long period of years.

Volume of business grew, and Virginia Can later became the United States Can Company, operating plants at Cincinnati, Baltimore, East St. Louis, Roanoke, and Chicago. By 1928 the latter company reached the position of third largest can producer in the United States. In the rapidly growing Southern trade Mr. Huffman's company occupied an especially strong position, which Continental has held and strengthened since the merger by locating plants strategically with relation to sectional demand. Mr. Huffman brought to Continental not only practical manufacturing experience but also a broad comprehension of the part which the manufacturer should play in promoting the welfare of customers through intelligent servicing methods.

About fifteen additional can-making plants were added in 1928 and 1929 to the Continental ensemble, and the Company took over two machinery firms: Seattle-Astoria Iron Works at Seattle, makers of automatic machinery; and McDonald Machine Company of Chicago, makers of metal-cutting presses and of the all-important can testers, which perform a most delicate operation in the automatic process.

Continental pursues and encourages scientific research with unremitting activity both inside and outside its own organization.

It has for many years contributed substantially to the National Canners Association, which organization has, among other things, rendered a constructive service in research and improvement of the products of the canned-foods industry. The Association is also the sponsor of the comprehensive work on vitamins in canned foods conducted since 1924 by Columbia University scientists under the direction of Dr. W. H. Eddy, which has resulted in valuable contributions to the knowledge in this field.

Continental maintains research fellowships at the Mellon Institute of Industrial Research, Pittsburgh, devoted to research on foods.

At Chicago, a laboratory with a large staff of chemists and technicians skilled in the canning art is maintained. Not only is research conducted in connection with the solution of Company problems pertaining to special enamels, lacquers, coatings, and so forth, for cans, but in addition studies are constantly carried on to improve methods of canning all food products. These technicians, as well as those stationed on the Pacific Coast and at New Orleans, Baltimore, and Syracuse, make frequent field trips rendering "on the spot" assistance to canners in the solution of their problems as the need arises.

Broadly, this organization offers expert counsel not only on better canning methods for packs of well-known products, but in the development of canning technique for preserving the newer or specialty items which are being added continually to the long list of fine food products available the year round in cans. A completely equipped bacteriological section is also at the service of Continental customers at all times.

In addition, the Company operates control and metallurgical laboratories at Canonsburg, Pennsylvania, and laboratories for chemical and mechanical research and development at Syracuse, New York.

In contrast to the highly standardized production in packers' cans, general-line can making develops many variations. The desirable container in this field is one which will help sell the merchandise it holds, and its success depends not only on economy and safety, but also on ease

of use, better display value, and all-round attractiveness.
A chief consideration is to develop cans which catch and
please the eye, while meeting adequately the practical needs
established by the nature of the product to be sold.

The Development Department of Continental studies
customer container problems from two angles. Does the
present container provide ideal protection? Does it help
to sell the merchandise? Failure in either respect means
that Continental suffers with its customer, while success
benefits all parties. Merely changing the shape of a container from flat to upright may double sales, because the
new article is no longer hidden on the merchant's shelves.
Adding an easy pouring spout to a tooth-powder container
may help a manufacturer over his marketing barriers. In
some instances the Development Department conducts
surveys of retail conditions as they affect a certain product,
takes the results to a manufacturer, and with his staff works
out a new approach to the market.

Recently Continental's experts, in coöperation with the
Dairy Division of the Department of Agriculture, undertook
experiments looking toward a new method of marketing
Cheddar cheese, as one way of relieving overproduction of
milk. Cheddar has suffered in trade because the usual
large, round units develop waste and deteriorate through
rapid drying and rind formation. The quality which gives
Cheddar its snappy taste, a certain gassiness, rendered
ordinary containers useless. By the invention of a valve-
vented can, an entirely new departure in can making, the
problem has been solved. In the top of the can is a vent,
so arranged that it releases gas at a low pressure without
admitting air. This unique package of cheese will soon
be on the market, the six months' aging process being now
under way. A new delicacy becomes available in a package

which ensures dependable freshness without waste and makes possible a complete guarantee of quality and trade identification. Other gas-forming products may eventually be marketed in this unique valved container.

Following the trend toward greater demand for tooth-powder containers, Continental designed a new can with an improved dispenser, making it an outstanding package in this field. The trial order for the above package was for only 50,000 containers, since when the sale has run into the millions. Many similar requests flow into the Development Department from buyers, with the result that this division must be alert to the trends in modern packaging. In the ever-changing picture of general-line can manufacture, a novel departure which catches on means substantial and steady gains.

One of Continental's new ideas, so new that it is not yet in assured production, is the window-top can, long a will-o'-the-wisp arousing keen pursuit but only lately brought into the realm of practical attainment. In the glass-top can Continental unites the protective qualities of the tin can with the visibility afforded by the glass top, producing a container which, while judged too expensive for universal use, is effective as an inspection sample. Through this method of display, sales of canned foods in certain test campaigns have been stimulated 300 to 400 per cent.

An innovation which rose to impressive volume within two years is canned motor oil. Progressive refiners realized that there was a vast market of buyers unable to distinguish between various grades or brands of oil. Taught by experience and advertising to ask for their favorite oils, they could not be sure of getting what they wanted. The fruits of extra care in refining, painstaking oil research, and strenuous advertising remained in jeopardy unless lubricants went to the customer in sealed and tamper-proof containers, the contents being drained into the crankcase under the eye of the purchaser.

In this conclusion not all refiners agreed, but it did not take long to convert most of the skeptics.   The first canned oil came to the market early in 1933, yet within two years over 200 oil companies were packaging a sizable proportion of their motor lubricants.   More than 65 per cent of oil dealer stations now handle canned oil.   In 1934, the second year, authoritative estimates indicate that approximately 350,000,000 quarts of motor oil were sold in cans, about one fifth of total production.

In cans the motorist gets the oil he wants and pays for — in grade, measure, and brand.   Dealers find these advantages : fewer complaints, cleaner and easier handling, and a reduced investment in stock as between a 55-gallon drum and a case of 24 quart tins, or a wider stock of popular brands on the same capital.   Lithographed cans, bright with color, offer the first chance to display oil attractively. Canned oil has sharpened competition by enabling the refiner to place his goods in thousands of new outlets, but at the same time has lifted the motor-oil trade to a higher plane.

A primary reason why canned oil caught on so quickly is this : Continental took its advantages directly to the public through national advertising.   Converted to the new idea, motorists came forward to demand canned oil, and the innovation became an assured success almost overnight.

National advertising by the can maker to the ultimate consumer was itself a novelty.   Hitherto, can makers had relied almost entirely on trade papers, concentrating on potential can buyers and overlooking ultimate consumers, leaving the latter to be cultivated by the National Canners Association (composed of food canners) and individual

packers. Continental joined forces fully with the canners
in these joint efforts to educate housewives to the advantages
and merits of the more than three hundred kinds of foods
and delicacies available at all seasons in tin cans and to
break down the old and unfounded prejudices against their
use. While continuing its coöperation with the Association,
Continental undertook to carry this work of education
further on its own account. Advertising texts and illustrations emphasized the point that health and freshness are
sealed in cans which preserve indefinitely the food values of
fruits and vegetables canned within a few hours after leaving the field. During summer months Continental called
public attention to the fact that, while Nature was at its
best, products of farms, gardens, and orchards otherwise
unavailable were being canned for winter use.

Acquainting the public with Continental as a service
organization, helpfully joining its own interests with those
of the many great industries which it serves, is another
objective of Continental advertising. As business develops
in size and complexity, producers of hitherto unregarded
elements in an assembled product are more and more seeking
a direct approach to a public mind appreciative of value,
cleanliness, and design, and increasingly interested in the
practical aspects of industrial coöperation. All these objectives have been realized; canned oil has already become a
standard product, housewives reacted favorably to the
messages on the uses and merits of canned foods, and the
public understands better than it did the part which the
tin container plays in the nation's mercantile and industrial
processes.

In its consumer advertising, as in other departures from
standard practice, the controlling thought is benefit to
Continental's customers, as Continental's progress goes

The mass production of tin containers involves an elaborate system of conveyers which carry the stream of cans through the various processes of manufacture

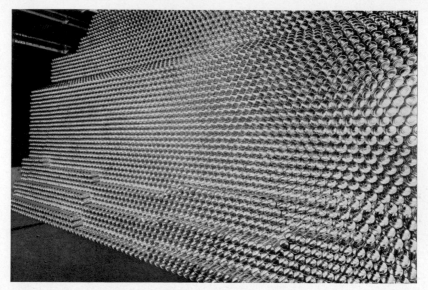

Gleaming like silver, this mountain of tin containers is the key to modern merchandising and the basis of its guarantees to the consumer

One of the Continental Can Company's forty-two plants, located near Chicago, at Clearing, Illinois, now the company's largest production unit

hand in hand with that of its patrons.   Alive to the wisdom of change, and alert in research and developing new products, in machine improvements, in anticipating customer requirements, and in advertising, Continental drives ahead with vigor in its efforts to stimulate the broad array of American industries which use its products in ever-growing quantities.

Unless all signs fail, the ultramodern store of to-day will seem hopelessly antiquated fifty years hence, as out-of-date as an old-fashioned country general store is to-day.   But one thing is certain : the store of the future will hold containers in ever greater variety than at present, and the tin can will without doubt still be an important factor in the commercial and domestic life of America.

GLASS ENTERS A NEW AGE

Libbey-Owens-Ford Pioneers in Adapting an Old Industry to Modern Needs

VI

GLASS ENTERS A NEW AGE

A HUNDRED years ago the United States Government wrote into the homestead law the provision that a four-paned glass window should be built into every cabin. Dedicated to improving the common lot of mankind, the young republic legislated against extending into new country the dark cabins of the colonial and pre-homestead era, some of which may still be found in backward regions. Glass is a civilizer, and it is significant that the first factory in the United States was a glassworks established near Jamestown, Virginia, in 1608.

Glassmaking is one of the oldest of the industrial arts. In our day it includes processes ranging from primitive to ultramodern, and products all the way from exquisite smallness to gigantic proportions. Here is an outstanding example of the rise of modern technics, not only because of the phenomenal advances in the art, but also because lowered costs and prices have brought an amazing expansion of the use of glass in new fields and markets. Once a luxury, glass is now a necessity, and the glass house of proverb has become reality. This transparent servant of light, which you see through rather than see, has a noble past, a dynamic present, and a future which enthralls the imagination.

As this ancient art developed into continuous large-scale production of the commoner forms of glass, both inventive genius and commercial vision were required. Particularly has this been true of the manufacture of flat glass, where new processes forced heavy capital investment in enormous plants and massive machine equipment. The march of the glass industry into new fields of public service and convenience, its competence in gaining new objectives by technical improvements, and its determination to reach new markets through advertising, are illustrated in the record and methods of Libbey-Owens-Ford Glass Company.

The three names which this company perpetuates are those of men who pioneered this change in industrial processes. All three died between 1920 and 1925, their companies being merged in 1930. Each scored a distinguished business success, and each met fully the duties which the Middle West, perhaps more than any other section of America, lays on the doorstep of affluence. To become a leading citizen in that part of America, it is not enough that one shall merely make money; in addition to building a fortune, an industrial leader is also expected to build up his community and country, promote good works for social betterment, and show a disposition, when necessary, to forgo the profits of to-day for the sake of the long-range future.

These three glassmakers of Toledo did all these things — each in his own way, however, for they were men of distinct and widely differing personalities. Edward Drummond Libbey, for instance, was a New Englander who, deciding to move westward his small glassworks from East Cambridge, Massachusetts, brought to Toledo in 1888 a deep background of cultural tradition. To older Americans his name is almost synonymous with cut glass, that beautiful expression of craftsmanship which reached a style peak in the nineties, largely as a result of Mr. Libbey's daring in exhibiting his manufacturing processes at the Chicago World's Fair in 1893. This success established his company firmly, and as his fortune grew Mr. Libbey, true to the New England tradition, used it to promote education and art in his adopted city. The magnificent Toledo Museum of Art, housed in one of America's noblest buildings, is largely maintained by a Libbey endowment, contains many magnificent paintings collected by him, and in connection with the public schools conducts a notable educational plan in art and music. Its glass collection is one of the finest in the world, with specimens illustrating all the changes of technics from the sand-core glass of ancient Egypt to modern pieces. Especially notable are a small Egyptian ewer of 1350 B.C., the famous Nekias cup of about 100 B.C., and a Roman cameo vase of the same period, the two latter timing the change from sand-core to blown glass.

In contrast to Mr. Libbey, "Mike" (Michael J.) Owens belonged to that rough-and-ready school of American industrialists who rose from shirt sleeves to leadership by extraordinary vigor in organization and invention. Coming out of the West Virginia hills poor but full of fight, he became a glass blower and labor representative in the Libbey factory. In a crisis in its affairs, Owens rose overnight to the superintendency, fired all hands immediately, and then rehired the more efficient members of the staff. His inventiveness resulted in the Owens bottle machine, which revolutionized bottle making by reducing to automatism an art which from time immemorial had required hand gathering of glass and blowing by human lung power into required shapes. His vision and courage are revealed in the part he played in bringing to practical performance the flat-drawing process, an equally revolutionary advance in window-glass manufacture, of which more later.

The third of the great Toledo glassmakers whose works are part of the Libbey-Owens-Ford heritage is Edward Ford, son of Captain J. B. Ford, America's pioneer plate-glass manufacturer. Edward Ford, retired as President of Pittsburgh Plate Glass Company in 1896, resolved to establish a glassworks of his own. Toledo offered, then as now, certain sovereign advantages — trained labor, access by rail and water to markets, raw material, and cheap fuel. Purchasing 173 acres on the Maumee River adjoining Toledo, Mr. Ford began building the model town of Rossford for employee homes and constructing the largest plate-glass plant under one roof in the United States, with a capacity of 6,000,000 square feet per year, later doubled, and now six times its original capacity.

As one views window glass coming out of the furnace in a glowing carpet at the world's largest window-glass factory in Charleston, West Virginia, it is a little difficult to realize that this automatic progression from melting tank to cutting machine is so new. Its birthday can be fixed in 1916, when the ideas of Irving W. Colburn, based on observation of paper making, were brought into practical use after Messrs. Libbey and Owens had spent more than a million dollars in developing the process, the patent for which they had purchased in 1912 through their Toledo Glass Company.

To comprehend the revolutionary character of the flat-drawing process requires a description of older processes. Casting of flat glass, in mediæval times, produced artistic effects still revealed in cathedral windows, but flat casting never attained commercial possibilities because of variations of quality, smallness of panes, and high cost. Better practical results were obtained by blowing glass into spherical shapes, reheating, and rotating until there developed

JOHN D. BIGGERS
President, Libbey-Owens-Ford Glass Company

Furnace hall at the Rossford plant, where the plate-glass batch is melted in pots. The batch is fed from overhead hoppers and ladled into pots through the fire door

a disk of glass marred by a bull's-eye in the centre. America's centre of production was Boston, and "Boston Crown glass" became a trade name in colonial America. After annealing, the disks were cut into small panes, those with the bull's-eye being used chiefly for transoms and door sidelights.

Larger panes resulted from another hand process involving exhausting physical labor and high skill, which came into general use early in the nineteenth century and continued to be the accepted method down to 1903. By repeated gatherings, blowings, and swingings of molten glass at the end of a heavy iron blowpipe, long cylinders were obtained, up to dimensions of twenty inches in diameter and seventy inches in length. The cylinders were then cut, reheated, and flattened; but the most skillful operatives could not bring to absolute flatness glass originally blown in cylinders. For this reason old window glass is slightly bowed and gives a considerable degree of distortion. Size and quality were limited sharply by human capacities under tremendous strain, and progress awaited a mechanical method for eliminating lung power and muscular fatigue.

The first step in that direction substituted compressed air in the blowpipe for the lung power of the glass blower. This made possible the fashioning of larger cylinders and sheets at less cost; but flattening the cylinders continued to produce the same defect until Libbey-Owens came to the rescue with the first workable machine for producing commercial flat-drawn sheet glass. Consistently improved through the intervening years, this process is the heart of the Libbey-Owens-Ford window-glass factories at Charleston, West Virginia, and Shreveport, Louisiana, both situated in natural gas fields. The Shreveport plant is the most southerly glass factory in the country.

Preliminary operations are similar to those in other forms
of glass manufacture, but they proceed on so vast a scale
in these great plants that a visitor may be puzzled in correlating the simple "shop" glassmaking of olden days with
this vast, automatic manufacturing programme. From
railway cars the raw materials are run up by cup elevators
into huge circular concrete bins, like farm silos, but much
larger. From these the ingredients of the "batch" are
drawn by gravity — so much silica sand, so much ground
limestone, so much soda ash and salt cake. These are
the chief ingredients which from time immemorial have
been used in glassmaking, but real progress has been made
in controlling the mixture in both purity of materials,
exactness in proportion, and thoroughness in mixing. After
these materials have been thoroughly mixed in a power
hopper, the batch travels along a broad band to the furnaces
on a conveyor system nearly a quarter of a mile long,
unloading being accomplished at any desired furnace.
There, with a certain amount of cullet, or broken glass,
it is fed into the furnace to be melted under a heat of approximately 2700 degrees Fahrenheit. Cullet, melting more
quickly than the new materials, starts the liquefying of the
mass and protects the sides of the tank from chemical
action during the early stages. Even so the tanks must
be frequently relined.

Eyes shielded against heat and glare by colored glass,
the visitor peers through an observation hole into a tank
of molten glass. What he beholds is a lake of glass five
feet deep and more than a hundred feet long, but the optical
effect is one of vast distances and weird, uncanny vistas.
The colors of this lovely, ever-changing mirage are those
not often seen on sea or land. Heat waves and convection
currents explain the illusion of distance and the diffusion

of light, but the layman will rest content with an unforgettable revelation of beauty.

This lake of glass in the great tank is ever being replenished at one end, and at the other end giving forth a broad carpet of white-hot, even-flowing metal. The endless carpet passes first through a chamber which cools the glass slightly by a short, sudden drop in temperature to toughen it in preparation for a straight upward pull to bending rollers, thence horizontally over flattening rollers, and into the lehr, for slow, thorough annealing. The powdered batch and broken cullet of a few hours ago have become fused into a solid transparent sheet; the white-hot fluid of an hour ago is now cool enough to be handled by cutters as it emerges from the lehr. The slow annealing possible under this flat-drawn process reduces internal strains and yields glass less brittle and hence more economically cut for glazing.

Glass cutting remains a skilled occupation, both in the manipulation of the diamond-pointed cutting tools and in the avoidance of waste by quick mental calculation to decide how a large sheet of glass may be best reduced to merchantable sizes and qualities. But even in this branch of flat glassmaking, which has withstood mechanical inroads longer than the others, machine tools march on. At Charleston, machine cutting is the established practice on large quantity orders, and the prospect is that it will supersede hand cutting to a large degree because of the machine's higher accuracy.

When you enter the great building few men are to be seen, which arouses the thought that men are being rapidly replaced by machines in this growing industry. Yet census statistics on manufactures show that 15,000 more wage earners were employed in making glass in 1929 than in 1899, a thirty-year period which includes all the major mechanical developments cited above. The answer to this apparent contradiction is to be found in the enormously increased use of glass due to decreasing prices, and cultivation of new markets for quantity-production glass. In this combined technical and commercial march of glass, labor shared to no small degree. The average annual wage in 1929 was two and one-half times that of 1899. Libbey-Owens-Ford hourly wages to-day are much higher than in 1929, and even annual wages are about equal to those of 1929 in spite of the shorter working day in effect under code regulations.

So far we have been following window glass through the ultramodern flat-drawing process. Now let us consider plate glass, the "blanks" for which can be made either by flat drawing, as at Charleston, or by the Bicheroux or pot method, as at the Rossford plant of Libbey-Owens-Ford at Toledo. In chemical content and physical form, window glass and plate glass may be identical; the difference between them is that plate glass must have further processing to produce the characteristics which give it superior market value. When window glass leaves the lehr, it does so as a finished article, requiring only washing, cutting, and inspection before being boxed for shipment, but when a plate-glass blank leaves the lehr it is still a "blank," semi-finished raw material requiring for completion even more work than has already gone into it. The blank must be ground and polished to close standards before it becomes plate glass ready for use as such, and these processes require both extreme care and large machinery investment.

On broad conveyors wider than flatcars and, like flatcars, moving on rails and in trains, the blanks, continuously bathed in water and sand which varies from coarse to fine, are carried under rotating grinders whose soft iron cores grind the corrugated surface away to parallel planes, thus eliminating distortion by taking off waves and surface irregularities. Then the conveyors carry the glass into the polishing machines, where, with soft iron oxide or "rouge" as a mild abrasive, the glass is polished by felts rotating at high speed.

On the polishing line you will see an impressive example of that union of power and precision which distinguishes the whole machine setup of modern glass production. It is known to a nicety how long those massive polishers with their whirring felts are at their best. Consequently an automatic crane at regular intervals methodically brings from above a new polishing battery whose felts have been reconditioned, and slips this mighty tool into place without a break in the movement of the gigantic ensemble. When you consider that this whole process is on a scale more massive than that of a railroad train, this marvelous timing seems a perfect triumph of factory engineering.

The surface, rather than content or thickness, distinguishes plate glass from window glass. The grinding and polishing of plate glass give superior clarity and uniformity of surface long recognized as a valuable factor in the manufacture of mirrors, in the display of goods in show windows and showcases, and plate glass is coming more and more into use in substantial and dignified residences. The "picture window," a phrase coined by Libbey-Owens-Ford and adopted by architects to describe a window framing an outdoor view, requires plate glass because of its freedom from distortion.

The most dramatic moment in a plate-glass factory like that of Libbey-Owens-Ford at Rossford, where the Bicheroux or pot method is used, is, of course, "the pour." As the furnace doors open, the beautiful yet awful majesty of fire is revealed. An immense incandescent pot of clay, holding more than 1500 pounds of molten glass, travels from furnace to rolling machine on an overhead conveyor. The contents spill out white-hot when the pot is tripped, cascade down between large iron rollers, and then continue down an inclined plane to come to rest as a flat, orange-colored oval perhaps twelve feet across by forty feet long. Power knives trim the oval into a rectangle and bisect it; then a door is lifted and the two great rough plates or blanks enter the annealing chamber and lehr, 450 feet long, to emerge 100 minutes later cooled down to the handling point. Then the blank goes on its way to the cutters, grinders, and polishers. The eye has beheld the glory of fire, and the mind has rejoiced in the power of man's thought to harness those titanic forces to his service.

When automobile manufacturers, about fifteen years ago, began building closed cars, they opened an immense new market for themselves and for glassmakers as well. Motoring became an all-year-round activity instead of a fine-weather sport. The utility of the automobile doubled, and the public increased its purchase of closed cars until they now form more than 90 per cent of total automobile production. From the start the automobile trade demanded plate glass, because of its superior beauty and clearer vision. The glass industry was faced with a challenge and an opportunity greater than it had ever known, since the call was not only for more glass and better glass, but also for glass on urgent production schedules matching in dynamics those of the automobile industry itself, which does not wait for laggards.

Obviously the use of even the best quality of plate glass, in a moving vehicle subject to collision, brought risks to motorists as well as blessings. Ordinary glass splinters on breaking; a shower of glass fragments is always dangerous and, as statistics of motor accidents show, often fatal. A survey a few years before the more general adoption of safety glass showed that more than 45 per cent of all motorists injured in accidents were cut by broken, flying glass. The search for a glass which would give greater protection to motorists led directly to the large-scale development of laminated glass, now generally known as "safety glass."

Laminated or safety glass is a sandwich composed of two layers of glass, with a transparent layer of some tougher, more plastic material cemented between them. Early efforts to popularize safety glass failed because of the difficulty of finding a satisfactory middle layer. Certain materials then available served well enough from the standpoint of strength when new, but colored and weakened with age. Absolutely clear materials were hard to get, and under the influence of the sun's rays cloudy and burned effects might soon appear which interfered with vision. Not until chemical engineers found means of producing plastic cellulose acetate from wood pulp or cotton at reasonable costs could the safety-glass trade reach its present proportions.

The laminating process is a delicate one requiring both high-quality glass and expert workmanship in assembly. After the plate-glass blanks have been ground, polished, and washed, they are cut to shape, coated with an invisible cement, and assembled with their in-between layer of cellulose acetate. Under great heat and pressure the three layers, two of glass and one of plastic, are welded together into a completed transparent sandwich. After being washed and dried, it is dipped in acetone, which softens the edges of the plastic middle layer to the proper depth to allow for routing out and making room for weather-proofing the edges. All edges are then sealed, ground, and polished to finished form, and after a final bath and inspection the completed product goes on its way to the automobile body builder.

The advantages of laminated glass have long been recognized. Visibility is unimpaired, and flexibility and strength have been gained. Safety glass may crack under severe impact, may even break, but the likelihood of cuts from glass is greatly reduced, as the glass tends to adhere to the centre sheet of plastic. However, it was not until quantity production and improved plastic permitted great economies and betterments that the advantages of lamination became available to millions of users. Intricate problems of design and manufacture had to be solved in laminated glass production, yet the cost of complete equipment in an automobile is unbelievably small. Nearly all automobile manufacturers provide safety glass as standard equipment, and the rest offer it all-round as an option at approximately $10 for the average small car. At present more than half of all America's motor cars are registered in states which have legislated in favor of safety glass, and 75 per cent of all new cars are being equipped with the protective material. With the continued encouragement of motor-vehicle bureaus and state legislatures, and the coöperation of the manufacturers, 100 per cent use of safety glass in the nation's automobiles is in sight. The leading bus operators have already seen the wisdom of using safety glass throughout their fleets, even in areas where no legislation is in effect.

Outside of the automobile field safety glass is making headway. All airplanes are now completely equipped, and the trend to safety glass is on in other public convey-

A 200-foot lehr at Libbey-Owens-Ford Charleston plant, where window glass is slowly and carefully annealed, thereby making the glass less brittle and easier to cut

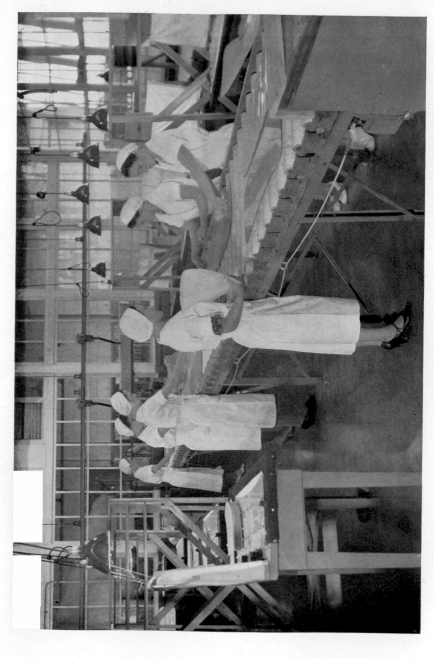

In the manufacture of safety glass, plastic material is inserted between two pieces of glass to form a glass sandwich, which is then laminated under hydraulic pressure

ances where passengers must accept risks not of their own choosing. The recent Century of Progress Exhibition at Chicago developed another use, exhibitors using it to protect their goods from theft in locations where close attendance by employees was impossible. Other uses will develop, as is always the case when a formerly expensive product becomes available at low cost through improved processes and quantity manufacture.

Emphasis on the safety principle in glassmaking led Libbey-Owens-Ford into another departure in research and experimentation. After obtaining the rights to manufacture in America "tempered" glass, a French development, and improving that process, the Company now is beginning to produce a glass which of itself possesses exceptional tensile strength and marked safety features. In the laboratories at Toledo the visitor can see a glass ball weighing nearly two pounds drop from a height of eight to ten feet, strike a pane of glass, and rebound without leaving a mark. When the pane finally breaks under greater impact, it shatters into rather harmless granular fragments, some of them no more than powder, the breaking process being that of crystallization rather than splintering. You can usually dash a piece of this tempered or toughened glass on a tile floor without damage. Two men can stand on a strip of this glass, which bends under their weight like a wooden board and then returns to normal position. In *Popular Mechanics*, Edward Teale says that a large sheet of this glass, one inch thick, will support a three-ton truck.

Tempered glass is made by reheating plate glass in electric furnaces, then suddenly cooling it by special application of air blasts. Europe is using this kind of glass for many safety purposes. Thus far Libbey-Owens-Ford has found markets for tempered glass chiefly in portholes for naval vessels, for which it seems to be ideally suited. Its use is also "indicated," as the doctors say, for table tops, mirrors, plaques, shelves, oven doors, showcases, and perhaps even show windows.

In the new age of glass so successfully inaugurated in the last few years, no single new exhibit arouses more interest than another Libbey-Owens-Ford product — Thermopane. This consists of two sheets of glass separated by a uniform dehydrated air space, the union being maintained at the edges by a dust-proof bond. Like laminated glass, Thermopane is a sandwich, but the filler is air instead of plastic. There is no decline in visibility. Until one examines the edges he is unaware that he is looking through two panes of glass instead of one, and it can be glazed in regular sash.

The advantages of Thermopane are such that it is displacing ordinary windowpanes in many better-class homes and apartment buildings. Air being one of the best nonconductors, Thermopane keeps out summer heat and in winter makes possible high fuel savings, estimated at 25 per cent. It also materially reduces street noises, which have grown to nuisance proportions in many cities. Thermopane is ideal for glazing air-conditioned structures, carrying control of interior conditions one step further, and considerations of quiet and health suggest it for hospitals, schools, and other buildings of a public and semipublic nature.

'Behind the Libbey-Owens-Ford organization, with its six huge plants engaged in making flat glass in enormous quantity by the most modern mechanical process, stands a great tradition. Its founders, in three distinct fields, led American glassmakers to new heights of accuracy and efficiency. Their successors, a group of men young in years but old in experience, most of whom have been in the glass business since youth, are taking a leading and constructive rôle in developing the new age of glass, one of the decisive phases in the revitalizing of American industry. They met the depression head-on and checked it, as far as their particular business was concerned, by finding new uses for old products, developing new products through research, and creating a desire for those products in the minds of the public through steady and intelligent advertising. The result has been more employment. Libbey-Owens-Ford payrolls, both in numbers employed and in wages paid, have been going from one new high to another month by month, in contrast to swings in the opposite direction in many other lines.

One sees in the recent history of this company the creation of a new large-scale industry — the manufacture of safety glass — and also a conscious acceptance of the responsibility laid upon industry to develop and popularize new products as a major contribution to industrial recovery. Internal developments such as these react definitely on the public welfare, and, being firmly grounded in economies, their cumulative effects are certain to be more enduring than external influences, arising outside industry, can ever be.

The Libbey-Owens-Ford Company's record in the last five years has been a dramatic denial of pessimism, as it has proceeded to develop, through new ideas and vigorous management, the great possibilities latent in the ancient art of glassmaking. Even in a period of general hesitancy, the policy of courage which dictated progress in adaptations, research, and determined salesmanship won public acceptance from a people always eager for substantial improvements in the goods necessary to civilized living.

SELF–GOVERNMENT SUCCEEDS IN OIL

*Standard Oil Proves That Corporate Business Can Be
Profitably Operated As a Public Responsibility*

VII

SELF–GOVERNMENT SUCCEEDS IN OIL

As a product of nature, petroleum is as old as the eternal
hills that hold it; as a product of man, it is so young that
one individual's effective lifetime has covered its entire span.
In point of time the oil industry is strictly modern history;
and in point of social history it is a large part of modern
history — an outstanding example of the power of applied
science and corporate methods to compass in a few years
a progress and general usefulness which in earlier times
required centuries.

The petroleum industry was born in 1859 near Titusville,
Pennsylvania. There, on a piece of flat bottom land beside
Oil Creek, Colonel Edwin L. Drake struck oil by deliberately
going after it, driving his well inside a casing to protect the
hole. Hitherto oil from the earth had been a rarity
recovered and refined in a small way, chiefly for medicinal
purposes. Drake's successful technique unlocked this
hidden wealth to the beneficial use of mankind. Since
his day $12,000,000,000 has been invested in the United
States in the industry he fathered, which now employs
more than a million men and represents two million stockholders.

At the start, few recognized the revolutionary nature of
the earth-punching in northern Pennsylvania. The Civil
War, then brewing, seemed vastly more important, and
until the war was over the nation could become excited over
nothing else. The oil boom began to make history where
the war left off. What a boom it was! Oil was better stuff

than gold, easier to find, easier to work, and infinitely more useful. All the oil in the world was right there in Pennsylvania, or so the footloose men of America said as they rushed toward the oil field. Cities rose as if by magic in the narrow valleys and on the sidehills of a countryside where, for several years, oil almost oozed from the shallow wells. Some of those cities and towns remain; others, like Petroleum Center and Pithole, third largest post office in Pennsylvania, have vanished almost without leaving a trace.

The pioneer producers wasted more oil than they sold, yet they sold enough to break the price of kerosene from two dollars a gallon to ten cents. One after another the rich fields were despoiled and abandoned — a melancholy example of the waste of irreplaceable natural resources under disorderly, untrammeled competition. Pennsylvania law held that oil was a fugitive and belonged to him who could catch it. The hunter had to get permission from the landowner to drill a well; but whatever oil came from a well belonged to its captor, even though drawn from a distance beyond his leasehold. Many a thrifty Pennsylvania farmer, expecting the oil under his small fields to be worth more later on, lost it all to neighboring drillers by waiting. Only recently has the country succeeded, in part at least, in overcoming the legal notion that oil is a "wild animal" to be captured and sold at will by anyone with the right to drill.

Meanwhile the pioneers were finding that it was easier to draw oil from, than to move it over, the earth. Lack of transport brought small refineries to the oil fields, while larger refineries arose at convenient shipping points. From fields to refineries oil moved in barrels by wagon over miserable roads, by flatboat down streams often so shallow that

WALTER C. TEAGLE

President, Standard Oil Company (New Jersey)

WILLIAM S. FARISH

Chairman of the Board, Standard Oil Company (New Jersey)

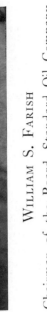

Fractionating tower and condensing equipment of a distillation
unit, for rectifying and purifying petroleum products

they had to be dammed and cleared in a series of mad "freshet runs," and by hopelessly inadequate railroads.

Then came the first successful pipe line in 1865, inaugurating a trend whose influence it is impossible to overestimate in the march of petroleum. Oil is the only great industry to develop and, with consequent economy, to operate successfully its own transport system, which carries the major part of its raw and finished materials. With the coming of the pipe line the oil industry — then, as now, predominantly American — began to evolve discipline and order.

The guiding hand in this organization phase was Standard Oil, a small Ohio refining company established in 1870 by the then youthful John D. Rockefeller of Cleveland and his associates. These optimists saw that oil had an unlimited future if its four great branches — production, transport, refining, and marketing — could be integrated. In production, waste threatened to interrupt the steady flow of raw material; transportation was unduly expensive and undependable; refining was then an infant art without standards for the protection of the public and involving great risks for both refiners and their customers. A market grown suspicious of dangerous oil products, both at home and abroad, required to be shown how to use kerosene and furnished with dependable grades. Uses must be found for those by-products of crude oil refining which were both heavier and lighter than kerosene, the more volatile elements, now the components of gasoline, being generally poured into rivers or otherwise thrown away, while the gas was wasted into the air.

A vast, integrated business developed on the basis of separate functions as well as of different locations. One Standard Oil company had large primary production and small refineries; another the reverse. Pipe-line companies operated no oil wells, while producing companies owned no pipe lines or tank cars. In the marketing field, some companies made special products but lacked both raw materials and means of transport. So energetically did Standard Oil lead this fourfold advance that by 1900 the various companies in the group were refining and selling the major part of the oil products in the American market and were almost as influential abroad, export trade having been one of its early activities.

As the result of litigation extending over six years, the parent company — Standard Oil (New Jersey) having succeeded the Standard Oil Trust of earlier days — was dissolved in 1911 through the distribution to its stockholders of shares in thirty-three constituent companies.

For a time the separated companies bought and sold goods and services equitably in an effort to maintain their position, but gradually, under separating ownership and diverging group ambitions, they became more highly competitive, until to-day all community of interest has disappeared. As for the independents, they had a sure foothold even before the dissolution and grew rapidly afterwards.

Standard Oil Company (N. J.), owning large refineries on the Jersey side of New York Harbor, faced the actuality of inadequate production and a too limited domestic market. Its great refineries in Jersey had been built chiefly to supply oil and gasoline for the rich and populous New York and New England market. Although large in extent, the New Jersey company's own trading area south along the seaboard to the Carolinas could not absorb the output of Bayonne and Bayway, where were refined the oils pushed across the continent in the country's greatest pipe-line system.

Obviously, the legal dissolution of 1911 accomplished its objective. The thirty-three surviving units set out to perpetuate themselves and to prosper, each as best it could. Whether the social gain of this change outweighs the economic loss involved is still debated. But, whatever the financial loss incurred through legal surgery, it was soon made up by the lift given to the oil industry by the swift rise to popular use of the gasoline motor car.

To understand what the motor car has meant to the oil industry, one must recall that until well after the turn of the century gasoline was a bothersome and unprofitable by-product of kerosene, the old, reliable, slow-burning fuel for lamps and stoves. There are automobile users to-day who have never smelled kerosene or seen an oil lamp. They may be interested in learning that thirty-five years ago Standard Oil, still trying to find a market for gasoline, organized a drive to convert the nation to gasoline stoves. The motor car changed this, until in 1915 gasoline sales surpassed those of kerosene. A waste product which the pioneers dumped in rivers or burned became the chief product, kerosene the by-product. As old Standard Oil sent salesmen forth to teach Americans to burn gasoline in the kitchen, so representatives of its successors now travel far and hard to teach the yellow, black, and brown races to light their darkness with kerosene, and at home to develop furnace oil sales through introducing improved burners for domestic heating.

The tremendous shift in demand from one fuel to another, with steady increase in volume sales, so expanded the market that there was leeway in the oil industry both for independents to grow and for disassociated Standard Oil companies to round out their facilities. But the free play of economic forces, continuing in spite of courts and judges, made for integration. Both the successor Standard companies and the independents, confronted with an unknown crude amount, were moved imperatively to seek new sources of supply, to ensure delivery of crude through pipe lines, and to deliver finished products through tank cars, tank wagons, and gasoline stations. Necessities of the situation drove dozens of oil companies to reproduce the plan worked out by John D. Rockefeller to bring conservatism and order into a business subject to flood or famine.

The hidden, fugacious nature of oil resources makes discovery an expensive and hazardous undertaking, yet the dependence of the world on oil renders that search imperative. Exploration and wildcatting must be encouraged sometimes, retarded at other times, but never entirely discontinued even though dry wells swallow fortunes or flush pools make oil almost worthless. We have seen how Pennsylvania once thought it held all the oil in North America. Then other states entered production — notably California in 1879, Ohio in 1880, Wyoming in 1885, Kansas in 1890, Texas in 1895, Louisiana and Arkansas in 1902, and New Mexico in 1909. Now the Mid-Continent, Gulf, and California fields are the quantity-production stand-bys. Gloomy prophecies of early exhaustion of oil resources have been confounded by the discovery of new fields, by improvements in the art of drilling through which levels two miles underground are tapped, and by progressive developments in refining through which a given volume of crude oil is made to yield larger proportions of those derivatives in greatest demand, at present gasoline and motor-cylinder oil. The "cracking" process and hydrogenation are cases in point.

As a result of these three forces — daring exploration, better recovery, and improved refining — America's domestic oil resources have been kept at least ten to twelve years ahead of threatened exhaustion. An extractive industry could accomplish that expansion only by vigor, faith, and intelligent integration. Conditions inseparable from the business of locating, recovering, moving, refining, and selling petroleum in an ever-growing market led both the present Standard Oil companies and their thousands of competitors along a definite course toward efficient integration, with the result that Standard Oil (N. J.) is now much larger than the parent company was when dissolved in 1911.

To Standard Oil (N. J.) were left two unimportant producing companies, Standard of Louisiana and Carter Oil Company; a number of smaller companies in which natural gas had succeeded petroleum as the chief output; certain pipe-line companies; refinery capacity beyond its remaining market needs and a domestic trading area large in extent but small in population and demand. In the foreign field its holdings were less constricted. Also the Standard tankers — the largest merchant fleet under one house flag — remained largely with the New Jersey company. Standard Oil (N. J.) stood forth as first in overseas trade — in exports of American petroleum products, in producing and refining oil from foreign fields.

On the home continent, however, Standard Oil (N. J.) needed to balance its operations before it could move forward. New outlets were required for the products of its refineries and increased field production to fill its pipe lines, tanks, and stills. In the first direction new domestic markets were developed; in the second, new crude supplies were added by the acquisition of a majority interest in Humble Oil and Refining, in 1919. With large proved acreage, Humble lacked capital for development, pipe lines, refineries, ships, and markets, all of which Standard Oil

(N. J.) could supply.   The New Jersey company is to-day insured as far as possible against lack of either supplies or customers, and transacts a larger proportion of the nation's oil business than any single competitor.   The Jersey group, which had 2,733,000 barrels net production in the year following the dissolution, had 47,973,000 barrels net in 1934.

Standard Oil (N. J.) is solely a holding company, a setup rendered necessary by the geographical scope and functional complexity of the operations carried on by its subsidiaries. Through these subsidiaries and affiliates Standard Oil (N. J.) is active almost the world over under different flags and sovereignties, each of which has its own corporation law and tax system.   In the United States, also, there are state and local regulations which make for diversity of corporate structure.   Then there is diversity on the basis of functions. Oftentimes an innovation may be tried out through a separate corporation more easily than by establishing another department in an already vast structure.   Thus has grown with complete naturalness a group of some four hundred companies in each of which Standard Oil (N. J.) owns all or a majority of the capital stock.

Close supervision of these companies in all their operations would be impossible for the ten directors who sit in New York, in spite of the fact that every man of them has grown up in the oil business and most of them have been with Standard Oil from youth.   Unlike many large corporations, Standard Oil (N. J.) has never expanded its board by taking in as directors leaders in other lines of business. The ten directors are working oil men, available for meetings every day; but, from President Walter C. Teagle and Chairman William S. Farish down, they know that the only way this vast business can be run satisfactorily is by selecting able executives to head each of the far-flung operations, trusting these lieutenants implicitly, judging them by results, and then correlating those results for the benefit of the entire group.

Peculiar aspects of the oil business make large-scale operations by some companies inevitable. Without them, the small units could not survive. From crude oil in the earth to gasoline in the automobile tank, large-scale production reduces costs, narrows margins of profit, and lowers prices on finished products. A pipe line must be kept full, and if the flow from one field becomes inadequate, another must be drawn upon. Refining is economical as a continuous process, but expensive when interrupted. A tanker can be efficiently used only if its cargo is loaded and discharged quickly on arrival in port; and the oil-burning ships now plying the seas require refueling from ports of call. The tank cars and tank wagons supplying the stations where motorists call for gasoline and oil must be kept moving. To anticipate and fill the demand for the oil products which make the wheels of the modern world go round is primarily a business for large and amply capitalized companies, and can never be anything else.

Consider the problems in discovering and developing oil fields. American oil consumption is so high, owing to our ownership of more than 70 per cent of the world's automobiles, that foreign oil reserves under American control are recognized as valuable insurance for the nation's future. Since 1859 America has been the chief source of the world's oil. At one time we produced 90 per cent; of late years the American percentage of world output has been declining and now stands at 59 per cent. Obviously American oil cannot continue to flow at this rate forever, even with the best of management. Other extensive oil fields may be discovered in the continental United States, science and effective coöperation may improve recovery and prevent waste, closer refining may give buyers greater fuel efficiency: nevertheless each gallon of crude oil taken out leaves that much less for future needs. Consequently, the United States Government at various times has urged its oil companies to seek reserves abroad, and through diplomatic channels has backed the claims of American oil companies for rights to participate in developments under other flags. Both justice and common sense dictate this course. Prodigally the United States has provided the world with a natural resource stimulating to civilization and vital to both social life and the national defense. Wise policy looks toward ensuring the return of like resources from abroad as they become necessary.

A case of this kind arose in developing the Irak oil field in Upper Mesopotamia. The State Department encouraged a number of American companies to enter the project. Before Mosul oil could be utilized, millions had to be spent in development and a pipe line 1150 miles long built across desert wastes to the Mediterranean coast. One by one other American companies, discouraged by the delays incidental to international control and mounting construction costs, sold their interests to Standard Oil (N. J.) and Socony-Vacuum. These two now share with British, French, and Dutch interests the 85,000 barrels of oil which the Mosul pipe line brings daily under the desert to tidewater. The American investment in the Mosul oil fields runs to $20,000,000, which indicates the size of the chips you have to buy to sit in on the international oil game.

Closer home are other examples of huge gains and losses: Venezuela, Peru, Mexico, Bolivia, Colombia — each with a different history. That of Colombia is perhaps the most colorful. The original French concessionaires were helpless

Stabilization and recovery plant for controlling vapor pressure
of finished gasoline to avoid vapor lock and evaporation losses

General view of an oil refinery, showing batteries of stills and tankage fields

to recover the wealth which, by all the evidence of geology, underlay their extensive acreage. The oil might be there, but could it be recovered and delivered where it had value? The site was an almost impenetrable jungle, lacking labor, houses, roads, food supplies, and even potable water. Merely proving the presence of oil exhausted the resources of the owners. They sold to a small American company, which in turn grew discouraged and sold to a Standard Oil (N. J.) subsidiary. The latter put $50,000,000 into the field and pipe line before it got a barrel of oil to tidewater. Standard engineers built roads, houses, towns, schools, pipe lines, and railroads. They sanitated streams to provide pure water supplies, instituted mosquito control against malaria and yellow fever, and built modern hospitals. Native labor, settled under superior living conditions, was trained by the North American staff. After years of costly pioneering Colombian oil began to flow toward refineries by pipe line and tankers. The task which had proved impossible for two small companies was conquered by a large company because it had almost unlimited resources.

Such developments make Standard Oil (N. J.) outstanding in international trade. Its foreign business includes 70 per cent of its production of crude oil, 50 per cent of its refining, and 55 per cent of its markets.

Immediate need for large capital also arises when a new oil field is discovered in the United States. With the shooting of the discovery well, newcomers flock in from all quarters. Houses, hotels, and highways are overtaxed. The rush for black gold and quick returns reproduces in a new environment the hectic scenes of vanished Pithole and Petroleum Center. Meantime oil may be gushing forth and running to waste for lack of storage or transportation. Humble it may be, or one of the other producing subsidiaries of Standard Oil (N. J.), which acquires leases in the new field.   Immediately that company starts in train a decisive series of actions designed to bring order out of disorder, profit out of waste, settled production out of flush production.   It shifts skilled men from other operations to the new fields, routes drilling and storage materials thence from warehouses and factories; and, if conditions warrant, begins at top speed to lay a pipe line from the nearest point on its great network, meantime endeavoring to bring the various producing interests into agreement on a programme to protect the entire field against rash exploitation.

With oil going begging at ten cents a barrel, producers have been offered much higher prices to win support for a prorated production programme.   Under an arrangement of this kind, producers agree to regulate production and to share equally in sales, and, by fixing upon a given acreage for each well, to abstain from trying to draw oil from under each other's land.   One well to twenty acres is the approved figure in many successfully prorated fields.   Then, subject to varying conditions, production is restricted to the volume of oil which can be carried by the pipe line and absorbed by the market.   By order of the Federal Oil Administrator in 1933, the price of crude at central pipe-line stations was fixed at one dollar a barrel of forty-two gallons.   Comparison of costs and prices in various fields indicates that in wide-open, non-prorated fields many producers lose money. Drilling costs are high because far more wells are drilled than are necessary; and production costs are high because the wells are of short life and may soon require pumping.   In the Oklahoma City field, where everyone went after oil on the principle of the devil take the hindmost, crude oil cost 90 cents to $1.00 a barrel, while in the Conroe (Texas) field, prorated from the start, comparative costs were only 15 to 22 cents a barrel.

From 1859 to 1934, Americans drilled more than 825,000 wells, 191,000 of which were dry, and from them recovered something less than 17 billion barrels of oil worth a little more than one dollar a barrel at the well. Accurate cost figures of the earlier period are not available, but those for 1900–1934 show an average production of oil worth $42,000 per well against an average cost of $25,000 for each well drilled, exclusive of prospecting, leasing, pumping, taxes, and overhead. These items equal the cost of drilling in most cases, so that it can be said that throughout the entire oil age America has been buying crude at less than its true cost. The operators may get back their investment and a profit in the remaining life of the wells.

The oil-producing states all recognize the validity of group agreements to conserve oil. Five leading oil-producing states — Texas, Oklahoma, Kansas, California, and New Mexico — have entered into an interstate compact to conserve their oil resources by rationing production.

From the consumer's standpoint there seems no warrant for disturbing the present balance of economic forces in the oil world. In 1920 the average price of gasoline in fifty representative cities was 29.7 cents. In 1934 it was 13.6 cents, a drop of 54.2 per cent. The intervening period saw gasoline sales taxes rise to an average of six cents per gallon; nevertheless the public bought its gasoline for ten cents per gallon less in 1935 than it did in 1920. This has been accomplished chiefly by improved refining and more economical drilling. A barrel of crude petroleum now yields about twice as many gallons of gasoline as it did fifteen years ago, and improved quality registers in better performance. Exclusive of tax, the average cost of owning and

operating a motor car mile for mile is less than half what
it was in 1920, a benefit accruing to the public partly through
improvements in automobile design and manufacture on
declining price levels and partly through improved motor
fuels and lubricants. In addition, gasoline and other
supplies of high quality are available wherever motorists
require them. These social dividends have accrued to
the public through the coöperative efforts of two great
industries operating under the free play of economic conditions with stern competition among their corporative units.

In this most intricate of mining operations, exploration
is spurred by possibilities of rich rewards. Each new pool
is the result of persistent individual initiative. Theoreti-
cally, wildcatting increases when the price of oil rises, and
declines as the price of oil drops. But the oil prospector
is such a determined individualist that price fixation on
any basis fails to discourage the gamble of drilling. What
keeps prospectors feverishly on the move is the possibility
that their luck may coincide with a period of high crude
prices. These price bulges come only occasionally, but they
are the lure which keeps exploration going at top speed.

Experience also reveals the difficulty of fixing a price for
crude oil entirely fair to all interests handling petroleum
on its long march from buried oil sand to consumer. Under
the dollar-per-barrel price, many refineries have operated
at a loss, competition keeping the price of gasoline, not
subject to regulation, below the price at which it can be
profitably recovered from dollar crude. To this extent
price fixation upset the normal relationship of crude and
refined prices. This is not serious, perhaps, to a well-
rounded company active in all branches of the oil business;
but it is a vital matter for companies limited to refining.
The situation emphasizes the difficulty of attaining com-

plete fair play by government regulation, however well intended. There is only one price regulator which is utterly fair in an unmonopolized industry full of unusual hazards, and that is supply and demand.

However, in this industry which has invested so many millions in the recovery of hidden wealth, the law of supply and demand does not now operate with the reckless speed that it did in the slapdash, early days. Then all hands sought quick profits without regard for the future. To adventurers with small resources, cash in the bank meant more than oil in the ground. At present, conservation of oil resources is being financed by large companies which can afford to wait while their oil, with that of others in prorated fields, is being produced and marketed in an orderly manner at prices fair both to producers and to consumers. No monopoly exists in the oil business; small enterprises are at this moment growing into large; and valiant, fortunate men emerge into leadership with every new pool development and every improvement in refining and marketing. But as the small companies become large, they inevitably progress toward integration and self-sufficiency, and tend to become conservative influences lending their weight in support of orderly and economical practices. Nevertheless, oil being what it is, a hidden and flighty substance which must first be caught, the persistent search of private initiative remains tremendously important, for without fresh supplies the industry must perish eventually. This essential balance is now the goal of the industry and to a considerable degree already has been attained.

The effort is frustrated somewhat by illegal production of "hot oil" and by the extreme size and productivity of the East Texas field, so large and easily worked that the controls applied to smaller fields have never been altogether effective there. But in the main the oil industry has of late years accomplished a tremendous work both in conserving oil resources and in providing the public with oil products at declining prices, even when general prices were advancing. If ever an industry has made a gallant and successful effort to govern itself, the oil industry has. From this point on, increased government control is likely to harm the industry without bringing corresponding benefit to the public.

UP FROM THE GRASS ROOTS

*General Mills Brings New Ideas into the Marketing of
Cereals and the Evolution of American Business*

VIII

UP FROM THE GRASS ROOTS

THE milling art is older than written history, and from first to last has been the foundation of a steady, dependable industry. On one side it is anchored in agriculture, and on the other in the everlasting need of the human family for the cheapest and most dependable food — bread, the traditional staff of life. Between these eternal bastions — land and life — stands the miller, performing an essential task which men have held in honor through countless generations.

In the long advance from the primitive hand mill of the ancients down to the great modern automatized mills, the power sequence shifted from man muscle to animal muscle, from animals to water power, from water power to steam power, and from steam power to electricity in the early years of the twentieth century. Meantime, in the 1870's came the purifier, and in the 1880's steel rolls were substituted for the millstones which had dominated the milling process from time immemorial. These two innovations, by improving flour quality and lowering costs of manufacture, brought disaster to many small mills laggard in introducing the new equipment; this period of transition is sometimes spoken of as the milling revolution, but it was a revolution beneficial to the public. Since then the milling industry has been steadily adapting minor changes, while inventive genius has found play chiefly in improving operations which prepare the product for market — packaging, conveying, and shipping.

On the map of the world the shift in milling operations emphasizes the sweep of American history. Even in colonial days large American fortunes began to rise on the solid basis of overseas wheat shipments from Virginia, New York, and Pennsylvania. These areas remained leaders in wheat production until the Erie Canal, opened in 1825, began to pour Middle West wheat into Atlantic ports.

Millers followed the wheat farmers closely in their march west and north across the prairies of the old Northwest Territory, and beyond. Wherever wheat was grown, a mill soon arose beside a near-by stream — the first industry to appear on the frontier. These small mills throve on local needs as population increased; the hazards of transport were still sufficient to make wheat safer to ship than flour, and the golden wheat of mid-America flowed eastward over the Great Lakes and new railroad systems to supply the rising milling centres of Oswego, Rochester, and Buffalo.

All through this period, exports to Europe were heavy, but ran more to wheat than flour. Wheat bread, the old Continent's basic food, could be made more cheaply from imported grains than from native grains. The Industrial Revolution gathered headway as European labor, no longer needed on the land, flowed toward the manufacturing cities and towns. Europe, doubling and trebling in population, extended its trade and political dominion on the basis of food importations from America. The Mississippi-Missouri Valley became the bread basket of Europe.

Throughout most of the area, wheat was sown in the autumn and harvested the following summer. This "winter wheat" became the staple of commerce. But in the Northwest, with its intense winter cold and long summer days, necessity drove the settlers to grow wheat which would mature in a single growing season. They developed and

James F. Bell
Chairman of the Board, General Mills, Inc.

Donald D. Davis
President, General Mills, Inc.

Batteries of roller mills, each containing corrugated or smooth rolls, which progressively continue reduction, sifting, and purification until flour products of the desired fineness and variety are obtained

cultivated spring wheat of superior hardness and good baking quality when ground into flour; but many years passed before Northwestern flour could be freely sold elsewhere because of its discoloration through flinty particles. The future of Minneapolis as a milling centre waited for the coming of capital, commercial enterprise, and invention, all of which played decisive rôles in winning for spring wheat flour a place on the world's table.

One of the chief figures in this great economic drama was Cadwallader C. Washburn, of a Maine family famous for political acumen and driving power. He came West as a boy of twenty, studied law and surveyed land in Illinois, and in 1842 settled in Mineral Point, Wisconsin. It is with the latter state that his fame is generally associated, as Congressman, as Brigadier General of Wisconsin troops in the Civil War, and as Governor. In 1856, however, he visited the Falls of Saint Anthony on the Mississippi River, present site of Minneapolis. Foreseeing the possibilities of this undeveloped water power, Congressman Washburn organized the Minneapolis Mill Company to control the west side of the Falls. In 1866 he built the first Washburn Mill at Minneapolis, the famous Washburn B, six stories high and the largest mill structure west of Buffalo.

The Washburn Mills went through several corporate changes before John Crosby came on from Maine to complete the trade name which has since become famous the world over. After passing through several partnerships the enterprise was incorporated as Washburn Crosby Company for $500,000 in 1889. This occurred shortly after the arrival from Philadelphia of James S. Bell, a third-generation miller who guided the Company successfully down to 1915, by which time he had lifted Washburn Crosby into an assured position with a capital of $6,000,000, soon afterward increased to $9,000,000.

During Mr. Bell's presidency the full results of the milling revolution, 1870–1880, came home to Minneapolis and the Northwest. The middlings purifier had improved the quality of spring wheat flour from 1871 on; introduction of steel rolls in 1880 speeded up the milling process and made quantity production possible without loss of quality. Washburn Crosby, in its remodeled B mill, was the first American mill to use the steel rolls, which it introduced after study of secret Hungarian processes. Entering its new flours in the Millers' National Exhibition at Cincinnati in 1880, it won the gold, silver, and bronze prizes on all three grades of flour exhibited, and a few months later adopted "Gold Medal" as its trade-mark, now one of the best known of American trade names the world over.

The milling revolution accomplished, it was inevitable that emphasis in the industry should pass from the problem of production to the problem of promoting consumption and sales. Quantity and quality were now assured; with close attention to details, products could be consistently guaranteed and the variety of wheat products could be increased.

Washburn Crosby realized this shift sooner than many others and met vigorously each of its several challenges. It pushed its foreign trade with energy, achieving greatest success in Britain, Germany, and the Scandinavian countries. During these years it led American commerce in securing revision of shipping regulations and eventually brought about an international agreement, signed by thirty nations, governing carriage of goods by sea.

Close cultivation of markets inevitably brought forward the advantages of spreading the Company's milling activities. Wheat is of wide variety, owing to differences in soil and climate; local tastes had become fixed and persisted in some degree even after wheat blending had become common. Freight rates, always of the highest economic importance in a business of bulk transport, worked against maintaining Minneapolis as the sole base of operations. Accordingly, Washburn Crosby built in 1903 at Buffalo what is now its largest mill, with a capacity of 20,000 barrels of flour a day, the first completely electrified mill. The site, long favored for wheat milling because of its situation at the foot of the Great Lakes, gained availability at that time as a result of rate changes in water transport from the Northwest. Another expansion era, in 1922, took Washburn Crosby into Chicago and Kansas City, the latter having supplanted Saint Louis as the key milling centre of the productive Southwestern area.

The Chicago plant and a later acquisition of General Mills, the Sperry Flour Company's plant at Portland, Oregon, have been developed particularly as specialty mills for a wide range of cereal foods in packages adaptable to changing diets and constricted kitchen space. The ample kitchens of Governor Washburn's day could accommodate his full-size barrel of flour weighing 196 pounds. Then came the cotton half-barrel sack, followed by paper sacks containing a quarter barrel. Now as little as twenty ounces of flour can be bought in a sack, and wooden barrels have vanished even in export trade. Specialties such as cake and biscuit flours — Softasilk and Bisquick — can be bought in packages of from twenty to forty-four ounces. Washburn Crosby makes and packages these and other special products at a cyclonic rate. On specially designed machines, arranged in batteries for rapid handling, "Wheaties" are boxed and sealed at the rate of one package per second on each machine, the contents untouched between oven and consumer.

From the standpoint of the public, advertising was the most evident reaction of this milling company to the expanding national market. Washburn Crosby began advertising Gold Medal Flour in a small way as soon as it hit upon that trade-mark. Ten years later it took the long leap of appropriating $40,667 for twelve months' advertising, considered downright wasteful by other millers. By 1902 its advertising appropriation had grown to $100,000 a year; by 1906 to $200,000. In 1907, in response to a telling phrase originated by its advertising manager, Benjamin S. Bull, the directors appropriated the then colossal sum of $650,000 to impress that phrase on the country. Soon "Eventually — Why Not Now?" had been linked with Gold Medal Flour in the mind of every American able to read. There is no rhetorical success in goods advertising equal to that achieved by Mr. Bull's swinging question, pushed by annual appropriations which passed the million-dollar mark in 1917 and ever since have been consistently above that figure.

Washburn Crosby led off also in making early use of radio advertising, its Gold Medal station — WCCO — at Minneapolis being on the air since 1924. In this, as in other regards, General Mills has continued the aggressive policies inherited from Washburn Crosby. Of General Mills' large annual advertising expenditure, approximately half goes into radio programmes. Flour and baked goods are bought almost entirely by women, and in addition General Mills seeks the ear of children; both housewives and children can be reached by radio more directly than by the printed word. Experience shows that the Betty Crocker household talks, the oldest continuous programme on the air, gain in effect by reaching women during the day even when they are busy with household tasks. By recognizing promptly the value of this new means of communication, this industry secured a favorable hearing which it has been careful to maintain by well-balanced programmes.

Marketing considerations led naturally to the creation of General Mills, Incorporated, in 1928. The cereal-foods business had become dependably standardized from the standpoint of production of staples; new trade and increased growth could come only from developing new products and securing more coverage for all products, old and new, through progressive merchandising and advertising. Part of the merchandising problem was delivery at least possible cost; in the vast area of the United States this meant manufacture at many strategic points and a network of warehouses covering the entire nation. The full benefits of national advertising could not be recovered unless the advertiser's products and services were available to consumers everywhere in the United States. Also, a broader spread of operations meant diversification of risk as applied to wheat, insuring supply against local variations of yields in quality and quantity. Accordingly, Washburn Crosby took the lead in effecting a merger, under which the new corporation, organized with a capital of $50,000,000, has bought the entire capital stock of the following well-established companies: the Red Star Milling Company of Wichita, Kansas; the Wichita Mill & Elevator Company, Wichita Falls, Texas; the Great West Mill & Elevator Company, Amarillo Falls, Texas; the Waco Mill and Elevator Company, Waco, Texas; the Kell Mill and Elevator Company, Vernon, Texas; El Reno Mill & Elevator Company, El Reno, Oklahoma; Oklahoma City Mill & Elevator Company, Oklahoma City, Oklahoma; the Perry Mill & Elevator Company, Perry, Oklahoma; the Larrowe Milling Company, Detroit, Michigan, and Toledo, Ohio, specializing in animal feeds; Royal Milling Company, Great Falls, Montana, with subsidiaries at Kalispell, Montana, and Ogden, Utah, and the Rocky Mountain Elevator Company at Great Falls, Montana; the Sperry Flour Company, the most important group of flour mills on the Pacific Coast, with mills and elevators in California, Washington, Oregon, Utah, and Idaho.

In assembling these corporations General Mills effected a consolidation of successful enterprises each of which combined a record of stability with present competence. It sought out executive ability and bought bricks and machinery as secondary to management. The history of each of the associated companies would be as meaningful as that already given of Washburn Crosby, but space permits only brief mention of their growth.

Royal Milling Company at Great Falls, Montana, established in 1892 by men associated with Washburn Crosby, pioneered both wheat growing and wheat milling in an area which has since become a banner wheat country, notable for grains rich in protein content.

Some of the Royal properties in the Northwest were combined with those of the Sperry Flour Company in 1929 shortly after General Mills bought the latter, the foremost milling concern on the Pacific Coast, with a history running back to the famous Gold Rush, the first Sperry mill being erected at Stockton, California, in 1852 by Austin Sperry and George Lyon. Six California firms with eleven important mills became merged in the Sperry Flour Company in 1892. Six other important mills were added later, and Sperry also entered Oregon, Washington, and Utah. This company now operates five mills with a total daily capacity of 13,800 barrels of flour and 1850 tons of feed. Its specialized plant at Portland can produce 300,000 pounds of cereals

General Mills, Inc., Research Laboratories, maintained in
Minneapolis, have made outstanding discoveries in cereal
chemistry which have improved baking as well as milling
processes

Corrugated rolls shear open the protective covering of the wheat berry, releasing the endosperm or inside in particles ranging from the finest dust to match-head size

daily. Storage capacities of Sperry and its allied Pacific Coast Elevator Company exceed 13,000,000 bushels at the five mills and eighty-eight county elevators.

The Kell group of four mills in Texas and two in Oklahoma; the El Reno Mill of the Humphreys in Oklahoma; the Red Star "Perfect Mill" of the Hurds at Wichita, Kansas; and the Larrowe Mills of Detroit and Toledo, specializing in animal feeds, are all notable properties manned by leaders in the trade.

Consolidating operations and disposal of excess milling capacities in the first months of its existence left General Mills with twenty-seven principal operating associated companies in sixteen states. Of these, seventeen conduct milling operations; the others are engaged in buying and storing wheat, merchandising, and other servicing activities. Total daily productive capacity is 81,700 barrels of flour, including bread wheat, durum, wheat rye, and corn; 5950 tons of commercial feeds, and 720,000 pounds of other cereal products. It has total terminal and mill elevator storage capacity of 36,424,000 bushels, and 10,498,000 additional storage capacity at 212 country stations. These tonnages make General Mills, which owns all the capital shares of its associates, the largest flour-milling company in the world.

No one knew the dangers of mere size better than James F. Bell, the founder of General Mills and its first president. Bringing owner-managers into the General Mills fold, he determined to preserve the owner-manager interest to the full by maintaining both decentralized responsibilities and profit incentives. Men accustomed to operating large properties "on their own" retained the precious opportunity to get ahead by personal initiative and ability. Mr. Bell believed that a corporation's best assets cannot be found set down in black and white on the balance sheet; they are the personal ana group factors of intelligence, enthusiasm, and aggressiveness which hold men of talent together as they move confidently toward a common goal. Rather more than the usual coördination of effort was required in the case of General Mills, because of the effect of one associated company's operations upon another. The problem was to introduce unity without decreasing the zeal of the various units, their executives and personnel in all ranks from top to bottom.

General Mills' decentralized administration is based upon men rather than upon property. Its ownership of associated companies is complete; there are no minority interests to complicate its financial statements, yet it accords wide powers to executives in the field and holds them to high responsibilities. General Mills does no milling or selling; those basic activities are left to the associates, each of which sells the products of other mills in addition to its own. Local advertising is also placed by associated companies in their territories. In these respects as in others, General Mills, by giving intense and continuous thought to the proper relations between a holding company and its associates, has evolved definite relationships which preserve local autonomy in plant operations while giving the entire group the benefit of national organization in matters affecting all the scattered units.

Division of authority between a central staff and decentralized units is one of the prickly problems of modern business. Too much centralization is likely to slow down energy at the rim of the industrial circle, where goods are sold and contacts maintained with dealers and consumers, where bargains are made and good will created by fair dealing. Too great decentralization means lost motion and increased costs through unnecessary duplication of effort.

Search for the correct balance between these forces goes on unceasingly in many large corporations, which swing periodically toward one extreme or the other. Not so with General Mills. Ever since its organization, a definite conception has been followed in dividing functions as between General Mills and its associate companies. A system of corporate government has been worked out along that line, under which men who formerly ran their own mills have been able to coöperate and coördinate comfortably and profitably, even in the depression years.

Before describing the General Mills plan of administration, let us review the background against which it was evolved. It is an old business in staple goods with well-established trade practices; at one time or another it has met all the crises and problems known to commerce. It has the poise and balance which comes of knowing that it is an absolutely indispensable industry, catering to a basic need of human sustenance. Style changes are so minor that they can be overlooked; the backbone of the business — flour — goes along regardless of fashion, and once a new cereal product has been established in the popular taste, it soon takes a place among staple wants. Moreover, the technical and mechanical processes, while by no means simple and continually being refined, are fixed in their main outlines and likely to remain so. The net result of all these stabilizing factors is to leave the leading executives of the milling world freer than most executives to concentrate upon organization problems rather than upon those of design and manufacturing.

No other business, as far as I know, has reached the point of bedrock self-analysis expressed by James F. Bell, Chairman of the Board of Directors of General Mills, Incorporated: —

"Our associates can be trusted for products; we in General Mills are selling results rather than products. Our primary functions are merchandising and advertising; on one side we act as a sales agency for wheat farmers and on the other side as a service agency for our customers — the grocers, bakers, and housewives of the nation. None of these groups are interested in flour as such, but only in what flour will do for them and theirs. The grocer wants turnover, goods that will sell. The baker wants flour which will give results pleasing to his customers. The housewife wants the utmost in nutrition and tasty diet for her family. Our job is n't finished when flour is sold, but rather when it is consumed; consequently we maintain a continuous drive to get flour out of the grocer's stock and the baker's bins and off the kitchen shelves to the table in forms appealing to the appetite. To do this efficiently, at low cost and to the general satisfaction of the consuming public, requires a large organization, because the United States is a tremendous market. General Mills limits itself to those functions which have a national aspect, but even those functions are constantly subject to review by the men in the field who are making and selling our products. Our aim is to give the maximum of help to our associates with the minimum of interference. So far this plan has worked excellently, during bad years as well as good. Under it our earnings have been stable and our progress steady."

The tasks which General Mills has blocked out for itself are entirely administrative functions. The parent company assumes all responsibility for finance, corporate records, national taxes, insurance, and accounting methods and policies. It borrows whatever funds are required by its associates to maintain a favorable position with respect to raw materials. Wheat flows seasonally from farms past mill doors, and this flow must be taken advantage of to save cross haulage with rising costs. This crop-moving period sometimes calls for large credits. A big, strongly rated borrower gets bank credit at lower interest rates in the national market than would be accorded to smaller borrowers in restricted areas. Each associate, with the advice of headquarters experts, buys its own wheat, maintaining a constant hedge to eliminate speculation from inventory account, but such outside funds as it needs from time to time for these market operations are drawn from the general treasury.

As previously mentioned, General Mills prepares and places all national advertising; in addition it advises associates on local and sectional advertising. Its Minneapolis offices place the buying orders on national contracts wherever lower prices can be obtained on large orders than on small ones. At headquarters also are centralized certain service functions manned by experts in their respective fields — research in food chemistry, nutrition values, and vitamin isolation; products control to ensure uniformity and maintain standards; a manufacturing service working on mill improvements; a sales service which recommends new merchandising methods to associates; a baking service for the assistance of bakers, which maintains, among other helps, a school containing the latest and most sanitary equipment that draws master bakers as students from all parts of the United States; and a packaging service whose results are open to all mills. Research departments are maintained at Minneapolis and Chicago, with scientific staffs at both places. The problem of distribution, particularly of farm supplies in relatively small communities, is a difficult one. Experiments in three major areas through the Farm Service Stores are revealing possible solutions. As a primary desire, a loyal and effective self-owned dis-

tributor is the goal in all areas. Where such a distributor
is not available, a careful policy of acquisition, maintaining
local management, is being worked out, all to the end of
ensuring to the ultimate consumer adequate and effective
service.

The central staff services originate and advise; they do
not force or control. The associated companies are responsible for sales and results all along the line; their own experts
in each of the above branches report, not to General Mills,
but to their own chiefs. This insistence upon self-reliance
all through the organization has received formal status
through the creation of the General Operating Board, composed of sixteen executives of the most important associates,
whose chairman is F. F. Henry, Chairman of the Board of
Washburn Crosby Company, Inc., Buffalo. This board
recommends operating policies and programmes to the
Executive Committee of General Mills. In responsibility
for origination of operating policies, this representative body
of executives approaches that of a Board of Directors.

General Mills makes another contribution to the enlarging
science of business management by definitely delineating
the relationship between plant executives and the central
or headquarters staff in detail as well as in general matters.
While central office experts are constantly in touch with
like members of associated staffs in the field, suggestions
from Minneapolis on which both agree go to the associate
company executive for approval or rejection. If the latter
formally accepts a suggested change in procedure, then his
decision, if in line with standing policy, remains in effect
and cannot be overturned without the approval or disap-
proval of the Board of Directors, which speaks on such
subjects through its Executive Committee of six men, all at
Minneapolis and ready to make prompt decisions. The

result is that General Mills has reduced to order and system many routine and recurring adjustments which otherwise might produce discords and inefficiency; and, as one administrative problem after another is solved, a system of procedure is being built by common consent to head off future friction.

The clarity with which these functions have been divided between staff and line, and the decisiveness with which division of function is maintained, make General Mills an outstanding example of corporate organization. Here is a clean-cut holding company which is determined to maintain local self-government in its various units and at the same time perform for those units certain all-essential functions which, in the modern complex of national and international business, they would be handicapped in performing for themselves. The President of General Mills, Donald D. Davis, coördinates activities as between General Mills and its associates, and as between the Executive Committee of the Board of Directors and the Operating Board. Although relatively young in years, his prior experience included engineering, banking, and manufacturing before he came to General Mills as Secretary in 1922. Since then he has served as Treasurer and Vice President, and in 1934 was elected President of General Mills, Inc., in succession to James F. Bell, now Chairman of the Board. Altogether General Mills must be reckoned a group operation in which many able men coöperate effectively; but perhaps Mr. Bell can be singled out as best personifying the dynamic, constructive spirit of the enterprise, with its strong, confident emphasis on the morale of personnel, while Mr. Davis is the one who brought its internal relationships into harmony and order by his keen analysis and orderly presentation of his company's objectives.

General Mills goes down to the grass roots for its raw material, and up to the skies with its radio advertising. It operates in one of the most stable fields of business, yet is one of the liveliest of American corporations in its point of view. Meeting adequately the growing demands of every stage in the development of their art, the companies and men in General Mills, Inc., have literally thought their way into leadership against stern competition. No student of American business practice can afford to overlook the policies and methods they have evolved.

WOOD, WATER, AND BRAINS

*Modern Paper Making and Merchandising As Revealed
by the Rise of Kimberly-Clark Corporation*

IX

WOOD, WATER, AND BRAINS

POWER, wood, and water are the essentials of modern paper making, and the greatest of these is water. The sheet on which these words are printed was once almost fluid, a fragile web of fibrous particles in solution, and the central problem in its manufacture was that of adding and then subtracting water.

It is water-born electric power which turns the giant machines of the mills, reducing an unending procession of tree trunks to their component fibres and then realigning them in thin sheets ready for the printer. The paper manufacturer uses more water than wood, more wood than man-hours of toil. All through the process, man supervises and controls mighty natural forces in the modern aspects of this ancient art, which was once almost entirely a handicraft.

Given water in sufficient quantity and purity, wood supply is the next factor in deciding location. The ideal site is on a rushing stream of pure water capable of being harnessed for electrical production and flowing through virgin forest rich in soft woods, preferably spruce and balsam. These are northern trees, and the farther north they grow the more dense is their wood content. So we find the paper industry of North America, or at least that great part of it which provides materials for newspapers, books, magazines, and circulars, concentrated in the more northerly states and reaching over into Canada. On the American side, some original advantages have been lost through rapid cutting of adjacent forests, and pulpwood is now carried considerable distances to the mill by rail, raft, or ship.

Once the lumberjack has felled a tree, it is sawn into standard lengths for transport — sixteen-footers, eight-footers, four-footers. For all-river work the approved length is sixteen feet; the hundred-foot monarch of yesterday floats downstream in pieces, which form part of a rolling mosaic of logs filling the stream from bank to bank. Here the rivermen — adventurers of the woods — shepherd the logs on their way, preventing jams, keeping the procession moving as they leap from one rolling cylinder to another. A log may float fifty to a hundred miles on some of those sinuous northern rivers before it arrives inside the boom-controlled area above the mill, from which daily supplies are drawn. After the spring run, when the winter's cut comes out on white water from melting snows, the river above the mill may be full of wood mile after mile. Powerful cranes and conveyors stock huge mountains of white or gray logs which often tower higher than the mills themselves as merely reserve supplies, to be drawn upon when water-borne or rail-borne supplies fall short.

The daily supply of logs floats to a jack hoist carrying the logs up through power saws which reduce sixteen-footers to four-footers. Next they lose their bark jackets, to emerge wet, shining, and clean, while the bark goes on its way to feed the furnaces, generating the necessary steam which later on disintegrates the wood and dries the paper. From this point the log's progress will depend upon whether it is selected for sulphite treatment or for grinding. In the latter case the wood is forced by hydraulic pressure against giant millstones until it looks and feels almost like flour. This pulp is then put through sieves and settling basins until all foreign matter and rank fibres have been eliminated, the purpose being to reduce it to an absolutely dependable filler material.

Logs selected for the sulphite process are reduced to small chips and cooked with sulphurous acid in a huge retort or digester. The result of this chemical action is, by bulk, approximately half cellulose, the wood fibres having become soft and pliable. The remainder is waste material containing lignin, still a relatively unknown quantity in organic chemistry. There are also in the residue appreciable quantities of resins and sugars. Both fortune and reputation as a public benefactor await the individual or group that can recover by-product value from these sources.

What happens next to these two materials — sulphite pulp and groundwood — will depend upon the product desired. The pulp may be bleached, pressed, and shipped to distant mills for use in paper or kindred product, or it may be macerated, mixed with the groundwood and other materials, and made into paper on the spot.

So far all these operations, proceeding at high speed and on different levels as logs are carried through the various stages automatically and as their derivatives in solution flow through channels and settling basins, have been merely preparing the raw materials for paper making. The latter process is a truly tremendous expression of science and power. Paper-making machines are hundreds of feet in length, and complex in detail, but the key idea is simplicity itself — to saturate solids with all the water they will hold and then get rid of surplus water as expeditiously as possible. The mix, perhaps only one per cent solid and far too thin to support itself, is flowed out upon an endless screen of fine brass wire which allows part of the water to escape by gravity. Traveling rapidly, the sheet is passed along from its wire support to a felt blanket. Meantime it is being subjected to intense pressure and cleared of water by various devices. It then passes over and between steam-filled cylinders and finally through highly polished chilled iron rolls which impart the necessary smoothness of surface to the sheet. Still warm to the hand but dry by ordinary standards, it rolls off the machine to become a gigantic spool of white, clean paper. When a roll has reached correct dimensions, agile hands break the web and start another roll so swiftly that the great machine itself is not halted.

Except for this sharp action, the paper makers in charge of a giant Fourdrinier [1] machine of latest model are inspectors rather than doers. From the moment the mix, thin as slush, begins its race through the machine, until it emerges as paper ready for shipment or warehousing, the work is all mechanical. But this kindly monster of a machine takes a deal of watching by sharp eyes and delicate adjustment by skilled fingers. In spite of mechanical and scientific aids, paper making is still an art, depending for its success upon infinite attention to detail at every stage of its manufacture.

As paper changes from liquid to solid before the eyes of the observer, the mind runs back to the beginnings of this vital business. The Chinese began it, say the books; in so doing they laid the foundation for the modern world, which has been built on the records of the past and the diffusion of ideas through the written and printed word. Lacking paper, history would be almost a blank; geography still a fable; poetry a harper's song by the fireside; trade a matter of simple barter, and the productive arts still

[1] Named for the English paper maker and inventor, Henry Fourdrinier, who at the beginning of the nineteenth century developed the first continuous paper-making machine.

under rule of thumb. Each generation, instructed only by word of mouth by elders schooled through crude experience, would have had to repeat in its own time the errors of its forefathers, and all human knowledge would have been at the mercy of precarious memory. Likewise, if these great paper machines should be stilled forever, our civilization could hardly rally from the shock. Imagine, if you can, the bleakness, incoherence, and futility of a world without books, newspapers, magazines, print of all descriptions. The survivors of such a catastrophe would soon be on their way back to savagery if the thought web which binds society together and preserves the accumulating wisdom of mankind were to be broken asunder.

In the July 1935 *Atlantic Monthly* Mr. Stanley Casson gives an archæologist's view of the inevitable disintegration of our great cities into rubbish heaps in which his fellow craftsmen, of some unnamed breed, will delve for telltale evidences of our vanished social life. But our best works — imperishable ideas clearly and beautifully expressed in books — have received world-wide circulation in such numbers that nothing less than a world cataclysm could destroy them or the means of reprinting them. Thanks to the art of printing and its sister arts, civilization is better insured against disaster than it once was; local misfortunes might force upon it a change of base and scene, but hardly more while paper continues to be printed.

Paper making naturally followed lumbering operations toward the Northwest in the busy, progressive years after the War between the States. That conflict, intensifying the demand for news, resulted in great increases in newspaper circulation in the older centres of population, and every new town in the rapidly settled West required its local newspapers and printing plant. A growing market for paper developed in the Mississippi Valley, and a swiftly expanding railway system permitted shipping to distant areas from the edge of the big woods where materials and water power were abundant.   Farsighted lumbermen saw the economic advantage of paper making, first as a means of using water power and timber not suitable for building purposes, second as a way to continue their activities after the virgin forests had yielded their choicest trees.   Thus central Wisconsin became naturally a paper-making area, especially in the Fox River Valley, blessed beyond other regions with abundant water of proper quality, large supplies of raw material, and access to markets both by rail and by the Great Lakes waterways.   For more than sixty years the Fox River Valley has been making paper.   To-day it makes more kinds of paper than any other section of equal size in the country. Paper is the life interest of this beautiful valley, and that interest has brought into being there the Institute of Paper Chemistry at Appleton, Wisconsin, supported by the paper industry of the nation to conduct fundamental research.

At Neenah, Wisconsin, where the Fox River, with the tremendous reservoir of Lake Winnebago behind it, begins its slide toward Green Bay and Lake Michigan, four far-seeing pioneers, J. A. Kimberly, C. B. Clark, F. C. Shattuck, and Havilah Babcock, began to make paper in 1872.   The founders were men of means accustomed to financing their own enterprises; they made no public offer of shares, and for nearly fifty years after its founding Kimberly-Clark remained a private, family enterprise.   During all this period the company grew through the ploughing back of earnings, remaining entirely in the hands of the descendants of the founders and a few active managers who had acquired stock interests.   Stockholders numbered only 52 prior to

FRANK J. SENSENBRENNER
President, Kimberly-Clark Corporation

Battery of the latest type of grinder for making wood pulp, used in Kimberly, Wisconsin, mill

the public offering of 1928, when the company increased its capital to $30,000,000.

During these years of small group ownership, Kimberly-Clark established itself on a solid base as regards both policies and properties. It enlarged its holdings in the Fox River Valley, where it now operates the Lakeview and Badger-Globe at Neenah, Wisconsin, Atlas at Appleton, Wisconsin, and the mill at near-by Kimberly, built in 1889 and rebuilt in 1903. Mills were erected at Niagara, Wisconsin, in 1899 (remodeled in 1916), and at Niagara Falls, New York, in 1920, the capacity of the latter being doubled in 1921. The chief products of these mills are as follows: —

1. *Book Papers* (Niagara and Kimberly, Wis., and Niagara Falls, N. Y.)

Kleerfect ⎱
Hyfect ⎰ Processed; for all printing purposes

Primoplate ⎱
Hyloplate ⎰ Non-processed; for all printing purposes

Rotoplate, particularly suited to the rotogravure printing process

2. *Wall Papers* (Atlas, Appleton, Wis.)

3. *Specialties* (Lakeview, Neenah, Wis.)
Cover stocks — Tribal, Economy, and Recondite Covers
School papers — Kimray
Box cover papers
Ticket stock, and so forth

4. *Crepe Wadding Products* (Badger-Globe, Neenah, and Niagara Falls)

Sanitary pads ⎱
Facial tissues ⎸
Handkerchiefs ⎸ Manufactured for International Cellu-cotton Products Company and sold
Hospital wadding ⎰ by it under the trade-marked names Kotex, Kleenex, Kerfs, and Cellu-cotton (not cotton) absorbent wadding

Kimpak, a protective material

Kimsul, an insulating material against sound and temperature

Sanek neck strips

Kimflex shoe counters, inner soles, and other specialties

The capacity of Kimberly-Clark's six American mills is 1,000,000 pounds of paper a day, exclusive of newsprint and crepe wadding products.

Extensive timber tracts were added, notably 200,000 acres of virgin forest in the Gogebic Lake district of Northern Michigan and Minnesota.

Under the leadership of Mr. F. J. Sensenbrenner, who joined Kimberly-Clark in 1889 and became the President in 1926, the company developed policies which were far ahead of their time and have influenced the entire paper-making industry. Recently Mr. Sensenbrenner's leadership was recognized by his election to the Presidency of the American Pulp and Paper Association.

In research in the always mysterious and still complex chemistry of paper, Kimberly-Clark has long been a leader, developing new processes and products. This was the first company to introduce reasonably priced rotogravure paper of light weight and high opacity to American printers; it leads in crepe wadding research and adaptations, and its work has been outstanding in improving groundwood papers by bleaching the wood pulp and by equipping Fourdrinier machines with special processing devices.

When Kimberly-Clark announced that in its new Kleerfect and Hyfect groundwood book papers printing qualities would be lifted to new heights at no increased cost, the printers of the country were skeptical, especially as to their performance in half-tone and color printing. The company not only proved the point in these respects, but by the new process developed sheets both sides of which possessed equally good printing surfaces, thereby overcoming in large degree an age-old printing difficulty due to the fact that the underside of the sheet revealed the telltale marks of the wire screen over which it had passed in the first stages of manufacture. The results are papers especially adapted to fast press runs in large editions.

In sales and advertising policies Kimberly-Clark recognized early the new trends in business. No Kimberly-Clark sheet is considered sold until it has been printed; once gained, customers are held as steady buyers for long periods.

In advertising, the company has taken its story to the public with marked success. By demonstrating with its own advertisements the superior appeal of rotogravure paper, it broke the ice for both printers and publishers when that field was new. Later, in introducing Kleerfect and Hyfect, a determined campaign begun six months before deliveries were possible made so deep an impression on the printing trade that these new papers were successful from the start, though introduced in the black year of 1933. These and other innovations, backed by consistent advertising, resulted in steady operations at a substantial per cent of capacity through the recent trying years. Kimberly-Clark is a shining example of the power of new products and steady advertising in overcoming generally adverse conditions.

In its relations with printers, Kimberly-Clark recognizes the paper maker's responsibility for performance as well as for product. Its papers are, of course, subject to rigid inspection, as are those of all leading mills. However, so varied are the conditions under which printing is done, and so rapid have been the developments in printing presses and inks, that the company maintains a close liaison with its printer customers through skilled field men ready to advise on technical printing problems. In this way it attempts to fill in what is by common consent the weak spot in the mechanics of publishing — the lack of complete and continuous coöperation between the best brains of the printing industry and the best brains of the paper-making industry.

In 1926, Kimberly-Clark joined with the *New York Times* in erecting at Kapuskasing, Ontario, a magnificent newsprint plant for its subsidiary, Spruce Falls Power & Paper Company.

Kapuskasing is situated on the Canadian National Railways, on the great arc which that railroad makes near the fiftieth parallel of latitude in its transcontinental progress toward the Pacific along the northerly line of settlement in the Dominion. The visitor to this industrial frontier has passed the northerly limits of established mining around Cochrane and Timmins, and is within a hundred air miles or so of James Bay, the southern extension of Hudson's Bay.

Coming by air from Port Arthur on Lake Superior, as I did, one flies over a beautiful wilderness of lake, forest, and muskeg for three hundred miles, a country almost untenanted by man except for an occasional mining settlement and prospectors seeking new gold strikes on this last of the rail-encircled frontiers. This is the greatest continuous virgin forest of soft woods on the continent, and Canada most intelligently is protecting it from fire by airplane patrols, watchtowers, and quick response to blazes. Burned-over patches are a common feature of the landscape, but they are mostly small in extent and traversed by fire lanes, each ribbed area proving that efficient fire fighters have there met the enemy and triumphed.

In the northeastern corner of this area the Kapuskasing River flows north toward Hudson's Bay. No one, save perhaps an Indian trapper or a white prospector, knows as yet precisely where this great tributary of the Mattagami rises, for parts of this wilderness are still unmapped. Here, in the Algoma and Cochrane districts, the Spruce Falls Company has under lease from the government nearly five thousand square miles of forest land. At Smoky Falls, fifty miles distant from the plant, stands a hydroelectric plant with a capacity of 75,000 horsepower, produced at the lowest cost available to industry anywhere. Completely modern because constructed in 1929, — and few indeed have been the paper mills built since, — the Spruce Falls plant can produce 175,000 tons of newsprint annually. Its location and equipment permit phenomenally low costs without cutting the corners on quality. Here electricity is so cheap that it can be used economically to make steam and cook wood. Here timber of superlative paper-making qualities makes possible an enviable percentage of yield and a sheet of outstanding merit.

No doubt Kapuskasing operations suffer from low newsprint prices and high freight rates, but their effects are not apparent in the town, a bright spot on the map of that far-northern country.

It is a company town, but, unlike so many company towns, it really reflects the Kimberly-Clark idea of what a town ought to be. After so much wilderness, and a bird's-eye view of some neighboring settlements which grew like Topsy, one rejoices that some central authority with sense enough to hire a town planner and capital enough to build with dignity and stability could establish this sightly little city on the flat prairie. From the air, Kapuskasing looks like a dolls' town of pretty houses arranged around a parked semicircle which gives upon the serpentine river that separates the town from the mills.   Three large structures — the first we saw in three hundred miles of wilderness travel — stand out as sentinels of urban civilization in the vast plain stretching away to the Arctic.   They are the Community House, the Inn for the accommodation of unmarried employees and travelers, who find there comforts long deferred in most of the North Country, and the Sensenbrenner Hospital, equipped by Mr. F. J. Sensenbrenner, an outpost of modern medical science serving a wide area.   Nearly everyone in Kapuskasing belongs to the Community Club, which, in a town of four thousand population, passes thirty thousand persons through its doors every year, offering them a wide range of educational and recreational activities, including bowling alleys and basketball courts, gymnasium, "talkies" (as they say in Canada), lectures, library service, musicals, home dramatics, debates, bridge, and, of course, tea, for this is part of the realm of His Majesty, Edward VIII. Perhaps the prize exhibit of the Kapuskasing Community Hall, and one indicating the good-fellowship prevailing in the town, is a lodge room which both Masons and Knights of Columbus, in all amity, use for their meetings on different evenings.

Because Kapuskasing was built from the ground up at one time, its attention to social problems is notable, but the Kimberly-Clark interest in community welfare is also expressed in housing and community club projects of similar nature at Niagara and Kimberly, Wisconsin.

While Kimberly-Clark made its reputation on printing papers, within recent years it has become a leader in developing absorbent paper products — technically known as crepe wadding — for sanitary, insulating, and other purposes.   Known to the public as Kotex and Kleenex, these

Dry end of huge Fourdrinier paper-making machine

Interior view of a Kimberly-Clark division, showing Kotex being made

are among the well-known products developed in Kimberly-Clark laboratories and made exclusively in Kimberly-Clark mills for the International Cellucotton Products Company, an entirely distinct corporation which advertises and distributes these products. The manufacture of crepe wadding from sulphite pulp is largely a matter of fluffing the wood fibre until it becomes highly absorbent, and to accomplish this Kimberly-Clark engineers have originated unique plant layouts. The highest degree of automatization and sanitary control marks the assembling and packaging of these and similar products.

Paper making is fundamentally a power-machine industry, employing relatively few persons in comparison to volume of output, but the continuous processes described require close attention and high skill at all points. Labor relations are consequently of the utmost importance. On February 18, 1920, when employee representation was a novelty in American industry, a council of employees was established to bargain collectively with the management.

This plan, revised as of June 17, 1933, contains more "teeth" from the labor standpoint, in the opinion of the employees who helped to draft it, than any other similar compact in American industry. The plan provides for local settlement of local disputes and for reference of general questions at regular intervals to a General Council composed of twenty-one representatives of employees from all the company's scattered plants, meeting with an equal representation from management.

The General Council, in addition to handling all basic questions of wages, hours, and working conditions, has legislated a system of standard instructions which govern the action of supervisors and employees in every important aspect of their relationship. Proceedings of the General

Council are distributed to employees, who are thus made acquainted with the actions taken, and apprised of the conduct of their representatives in joint conference with management. The employees have equal voice not only in determining wages and hours, but also in many other matters commonly reserved to management. For instance, the councils are now working out together with the management a complete job analysis and classification under which wage rates will be set in accordance with the relative importance of each job. Just as Kimberly-Clark acted on collective bargaining long before government acted in that field, so the management of the Corporation announced to employees, on the downfall of the NRA, that no changes will be made in any relationship except through joint action in General Council. "Our agreements with employees under the Council plan," said President Sensenbrenner, "are as binding on us as they would be under the law."

There seems to exist in Kimberly-Clark a desire on the part of both management and representatives of employees to be worthy of the other's respect. They realize that law alone cannot compel right relations within industry. That must be achieved from the inside out, rather than from the outside in. They have evidently built on the theory that both parties to a collective-bargaining enterprise must contribute their share of good will, patience, and respect for personality. In spite of many controversial issues which must necessarily exist under the prevailing wage and profit system, employees and management of Kimberly-Clark seem to have got hold of those basic elements of common interest which are so frequently lost sight of in modern industrial life.

In the cities where it is a leading industrial factor, Kimberly-Clark has built clubhouses, swimming pools, and hospitals, and in some cases provides housing; but the operation of these properties is inside the sphere of labor relations, and employees join in establishing the rates and rules under which these facilities are used. It would be difficult to find a more cohesive and intelligent labor force, the coöperative spirit having been built up by years of fair dealing, steady employment, and the long-established practice of joint conferences between management and men.

In Kimberly-Clark the observer will note certain characteristics which are the natural result of its long existence as a family or small group enterprise. There is a deep concern for quality output and customer satisfaction; also a fraternal note in its relations with employees, most of whom live in relatively small cities where Kimberly-Clark itself furnishes practically all the jobs.

In the reach of its research, engineering, industrial relations, advertising, and sales promotion activities, Kimberly-Clark Corporation is as alert and progressive as any business unit in the country, regardless of size or reputation. It has moved confidently forward in the seven years since it became listed on the New York Stock Exchange, and the prospects are bright for its continued leadership in the many important branches of paper making in which it specializes.

MODERNIZING THE BUILDING INDUSTRY

Johns-Manville Thinks Its Way through the Tangle of Construction

X

MODERNIZING THE BUILDING INDUSTRY

THE constructive point of view that corporate profits flow from consumer satisfaction and public good will can fairly be said to dominate in many important fields of American business. This is common in industries which place their products in the consumer's hands as complete units ready for use, to be tested in performance under conditions where the purchaser is a proper judge of quality, as in the case of automobiles. It is less frequently found among producers of goods which are merged with other goods and thereafter cannot be easily identified by the layman — structural materials, for example, which are of many sorts, come from scattered sources and are frequently hidden in the completed structure. Yet in this very field one finds in the Johns-Manville Corporation an acceptance and application of a concept of business which lifts this company well above the horizon of an industry decisively in need of a constructive example of this sort as it struggles to raise shelter to a new dignity and significance in the social order.

Even a casual glance reveals the building industry as lagging in the march toward consumer satisfaction and at its worst in the single family home, precisely where efficient production would most benefit society. In larger structures — notably office buildings, apartment buildings, and factories — there have been marked advances in assembling materials and speeding construction by machine aids. New materials, undreamed of in earlier days and applicable alike to large structures and small, have effected advances in durability, cleanliness, economy, quiet, and safety. For many of the latter Johns-Manville is responsible. It began by introducing asbestos to the American building industry and has gone on to develop a host of other dependable innovations, providing fireproof roofing and walls, insulations against heat and cold, control of sound, and low maintenance costs. Despite these new factors, the building of a home, usually a family man's largest undertaking financially and certainly his most important contribution to social stability and the future of his country, remains unnecessarily difficult, expensive, and soul-racking.

Home building has changed little in essentials since the beginning of America. Its chief materials and the craftsmanship which joins these materials together are fundamentally those the Pilgrims used three hundred years ago. Details have altered, but the basic conception holds. In housing there has been no revolutionary leap comparable to the shift from horse-drawn vehicles to automotive transport, or that in food habits which followed large-scale canning, packaging, and automatic refrigeration. To this day no customer can tell in advance what the cost of his completed house will be, if one considers everything in the housing equation from raw land to grading and planting after the dwelling is finished. The odds are that it will cost more than the estimates and that from first to last there will be enough delays and disputes to dishearten the budding proprietor. What he owns, after the worst is over, is not a guaranteed house, but one on which he must assume considerable risk in directions beyond his knowledge during construction.

These difficulties inhere in the stubborn fact that most houses are tailor-made jobs. Not only are the plans different (standardization is yet an American ideal in housing), but they are executed under widely varying conditions by personnel changing from job to job and sometimes from day to day. The average building craftsman is employed no more than five months a year. Seasonal nature of the work and inefficiency of coöperation during the relatively short periods of joint effort tend to lift costs. As a result some who crave houses cannot afford the great adventure of building, and others who can afford it refuse to enter upon the expensive uncertainties necessary to realize their dreams.

Because the materials involved are so many and the interests behind them so highly competitive, few consistent efforts have been made to vitalize into active demand the widespread desire for better housing. The 400 or 500 manufacturers of building materials, operating 49,000 factories in the United States, do not work together to sell the public the idea of better shelter. The industry thinks less in terms of ultimate consumers than in terms of middlemen — chiefly contractors and supply men — who place the orders. Missionary work in favor of homemaking is left largely to realtors and speculative builders who must charge high rates for their services because of the heavy risks they assume between purchase and sale. As a result the construction chain breaks at its weakest point; when housing demand falls off, the decline can be dismal indeed. In the recent depression the building industry registered the rock-bottom low of all business, total construction falling from $10,000,000,000 in 1928 to $2,500,000,000 in 1934, and residential building from $2,800,000,000 to $250,000,000 — the latter more than 90 per cent off.

Obviously many causes contribute to this weakness, an important one being the fact that nearly every housebuilding operation involves a loan. More will be said upon this subject later. However, I think that lack of stability and cohesion within itself is the chief difficulty of the building industry and that this flows directly from its relative inability to think in terms of the ultimate consumer.

So important is this point of view as an approach to an understanding of modern business that examples at either end of the scale may be illuminating. At the lowest rung of the ladder leading to popular favor stands the gray-goods division of the cotton textile industry, which with one or two signal exceptions has turned its customer contacts over to the processors. As a result the general public turns a deaf ear when the gray-goods people recount their sorrows. Textiles, as an industry, suffer under what the diplomats call a bad press, and gray goods has no press at all, because its leaders have never cultivated their public.

On the other hand, consider the automobile industry, with which Johns-Manville is intimately associated as a leading manufacturer of brake linings. Not only do automobile manufacturers cohere on broad objectives of wide human interest, such as good roads and safety campaigns; they also acutely cultivate consumer satisfaction. To prospects they offer, under effective guarantees, standardized products at stipulated prices with nothing left to vagaries of estimate. If the buyer does not pay on the nail, he is accommodated with credit for a definite period at fixed rates, on a schedule of payments calculated to discharge his debt while the security is still good. The local credit situation means everything to a home buyer, nothing to an automobile buyer. Consumer preference in automobile styling is carefully studied; even luxury appointments may be included in the amount on the price tag. Behind all this, and properly dramatized for public interest, lies a stirring history of technical advance, good reading for a mechanically-minded people. From raw material to finished product, industrial

LEWIS H. BROWN

President, Johns-Manville Corporation

An aerial photograph of the huge plant of the Johns-Manville Corporation at Manville, New Jersey — one of eleven plants operated by this company

control in automobiledom aims primarily at consumer good will.

Contrast this picture with the situation which begins to unfold the moment a consumer goes into the market to buy, not a unit of transportation, but a unit of shelter. When Mr. Citizen purchased his automobile, he did so in a single transaction. This is impossible in house buying unless one deals with a developer or speculative builder, in which case the buyer accepts something which is not always precisely what he wants.

A house is an assembly of from thirty to fifty different sorts of structural materials, fixtures, and equipment, each fabricated and marketed by an independent concern and purchased more or less over the counter at retail. These materials are brought to the site and put together by two to a dozen subcontractors. Each subcontractor naturally holds out for his legal rights and insists on favorable working conditions not always obtainable in the hurly-burly of present building, and his prior agreements with his labor may interfere with most efficient coöperation with other workers on the job. Inherent in this loose-jointed, catch-as-catch-can handling of materials, processes, labor, and executive responsibilities, are possibilities of disappointment which materialize all too often — failure to complete and deliver the house on time, according to specifications, and at a price corresponding to the original estimate. In the end the house buyer is almost sure to find that he has paid for his unit of shelter a price badly out of line with the value he is accustomed to receive at the hands of many industries whose processes, all the way from raw material to ultimate form, have been subject to rationalized industrial control, and whose products and prices represent more or less a consumer's dividend on large-scale fabrication and efficient management. In a word, when we set out to buy food, clothing, fuel, transportation, or amusement, we buy in a 1936 market under 1936 conditions, prices, guarantees, and trade customs; but when we set out to buy shelter in its commonest form, there is a throw-back to values, prices, conditions of purchase, and buyer's risks not essentially unlike those which obtained in Colonial America more than a century and a half ago.

Of course there are valid reasons for this continued backwardness. Housing is ultimately connected with ways of life in which tradition runs exceptionally strong. The house has become an ideal as well as a reality, and radical changes arouse disfavor as challenging something almost sacred. Consequently, there has been little consumer encouragement to fundamental improvement. The home owner has seldom been sure of what he wanted, partly because he was not aware of what he could get.

It is idle to stress the home's superiority over the motor car as a character-building agency and a stabilizing force in society, until convenience in acquiring the two is comparable. Obviously, correction is difficult, since no quick revolution can be expected in an old trade. The best that can be looked for is fairly rapid evolution which will gain headway as other elements in the industry follow the lead of Johns-Manville across the threshold of continuous thought on the consumer's end of the housebuilding equation. No one can say precisely how the vast but now slumbrous building industry will be revived and revitalized. To-day frank discussion can go on amid general approval, for all the lively minds in the industry are aware that a crisis has been reached out of which the industry cannot pull itself by its bootstraps. The competition is no longer between this material and that, this builder and that, but between

home-owning life and other ways of life, with the home-owning life at a disadvantage.

To overcome this disadvantage will require a sturdy
bridge of thought between old ways and new objectives.
It is a long crossing; and before it can even be attempted
someone must discern the promised land on the distant
shore, question the long-accepted limitations on length of
span, make a survey to locate firm bases for the carry-over,
and sound the rallying cry for all concerned to assist. This
Johns-Manville has done and is doing. For years it has
been financing significant studies and fact-finding surveys
on the history and economics of building, the needs and
desires of consumers, and the complex trade factors which
create the sad lag between the potential desire for home
creation and the shrunken materialization of that desire.
This corporation has carried through statistical labors which
contribute to promising developments in housing, revival
of the building industry, satisfaction of consumers, and the
welfare of future generations. Johns-Manville can tell you
what it cost your great-great-grandfather to build the old
family homestead in 1786, or what his ancestors paid for
labor and materials in England back to 1601; how building costs rose and fell decade by decade, with due allowance
for the changing value of money; and how the sectional
variations inevitable in a vast country like America affect
prices. Another large-scale study examined the house-
financing system of Germany, France, and England to
determine what features of their experience should be
incorporated into American practice. This statistical
spade-work, so necessary for building a case for basic
change in an industry inclined to let well enough alone,
called not only for vision but for a determined pursuit of
truth.

If you ask what Johns-Manville stands to recover from this research, the answer is clear. Being one of the greatest fabricators of building materials of wide range and adaptability, whatever tends to revive building and place that industry in a strong, go-ahead position must inevitably react to Johns-Manville's advantage. This is the more certain to be the case because Johns-Manville, from 1858 on, has been introducing to the trade products which were essentially novelties to the building craftsmen and house buyers. It began with asbestos, that cheap mineral notable for its fire-resistant qualities and which is now a component of many products in a wide variety of forms. To-day one finds asbestos mixed with cement in transite and other J-M wallboards, strong and fireproof; in shingles of many varieties and prices; in transite pipe, which is proof against ordinary corrosive conditions and electrolysis; in sound-absorbing and quiet-producing interiors, and many other products which, hidden from sight, give quality to a structure. Asbestos is a material with unique chemical and physical properties peculiarly valuable in building; the task was to adapt it to construction. Success with asbestos stimulated laboratory research looking toward the effective use of other low-priced raw materials whose properties recommended their use in shelters. Among these was rock-wool home insulation, to name only one of the many substances which J-M laboratories have brought into new, merchantable form. Experience in developing and marketing new products has given this corporation the courage to strike out in new paths; its whole history has been of discovery and pioneering. But along with the risk of innovation went corresponding benefits. J-M products were novelties easily identified and not easily copied. Consistent advertising established them before copying could become effective; alert manufacturing and fair merchandising policies have since solidified its position so that any building revival must bring it substantial benefits. Consequently whatever Johns-Manville has spent in its investigations of building conditions beneficial to the entire industry may be considered a long-term investment on which, in the very nature of things, it can hardly fail to recover adequate return. Beyond that, the strengthening of its leadership in a forward movement is one of those potent intangibles which stimulate a business group from top to bottom and at the same time interest a wide audience of intelligent and influential persons.

Even a slight reading of history offers proof that the masses of men are better found than of old, and the chief reason for this material betterment must lie in the fact that labor's purchasing power has increased. In other words, goods have cheapened in terms of toil. Productivity has multiplied through invention and discovery, research, machine technics, mass production, industrial control. Of all the major industries, not excluding agriculture, building felt this quickening impulse the least. Consequently it is not surprising that at last the building industry is attempting to stabilize itself by following precedents effective in other lines. As an indication of the progress being made, the cost of new dwellings has declined almost 25 per cent since 1926, and the home of to-day contains more labor-saving and comfort-giving devices than that of 1926. This is due not only to lower wages and material costs, but also to increased efficiency in construction.

"Prefabrication" is the term which the industry has adopted to describe this trend, or perhaps it would be more correct to say that this rather loose term has been tacked to the new movement by amateurs and publicists without the whole-hearted consent of the professionals. At any rate, Johns-Manville does not believe that prefabricated housing is a complete, ready-made answer to the complicated problems we are examining. Notable steps are being taken in that direction, but if anyone expects the housing problem to be solved at all soon by mass-production methods, let him take counsel of patience and listen to some of the reservations which require to be made in the interests of conservatism.

In the first place a house can never be shipped as a package. Difficulties of transport, bulk of materials, and variety of local conditions force assembly at the site. No house can be bought as a thing apart from the land it is destined to occupy, as an automobile can be bought after it comes off the line in a factory where every step in the assembly has been under one management in a controlled environment. The utmost tenable hope of the most ardent champion of complete prefabrication is that house parts will be made in their factories of origin with more regard to ultimate economical use, transported with less delay, put together with greater efficiency by men better trained in coöperation under management capable of doing an expeditious job according to plan, all the way from excavation to landscaping, to the end that the buyer will receive a completely built, serviced, insulated, sanitated, decorated, electrified, and perhaps also furnished dwelling at an agreed price. This fascinating prospect has stimulated the public mind to new interest in housing, but like most of the happy and hearty ideals of mankind it will be a long time maturing. Nothing like the Utopian programme described above could be realized at once if the whole building industry should suddenly see a great light and move with one accord toward that great objective. Neither the means nor the materials are available; the organization necessary would require years of training; and, most important of all, the customers are not yet ready to buy ready-made houses in quantity.

Tradition works directly for variety in housing. The human spirit craves a dwelling place which reflects individuality. Of course this preference will not stand up forever, if and when prefabrication offers amazingly better values; but a desire so deep-seated may be long a-dying, and in the meantime the building industry must live. What it will do, and is now beginning to do, is to proceed step by step toward prefabrication, expecting that in the future a balance will be struck between factors and forces now in collision. Buyers may come to accept greater uniformity to acquire enhanced values, or fabricators and their architects may find ways of satisfying personal desires to a considerable degree without breaking the chain of orderly, efficient construction.

First steps in this progression are clear. One is prefabrication of materials in such wise that their use at the site makes construction more efficient. At this point Johns-Manville concentrates its immediate energies while looking ahead to more comprehensive developments. Other manufacturers are striving in the same direction; present heavy wastage of materials is sure to be greatly reduced.

Another advance is the relatively complete prefabrication of portions of homes. Even the most ardent individualist in housing will hardly object to a standardized kitchen, because the kitchen is essentially a workroom where labor saving is more important than expression of personality or support of a mood. Consequently assemblies of kitchen equipment are "breaking the ice" for prefabrication. By such acquaintanceships the public will gradually adjust itself to a new order in housing. In some parts of the country and in some lines of building, acceptance may come more quickly than in others. Nevertheless, tradition against uniformity and novel designs will pass slowly enough to render the change evolutionary rather than revolutionary.

So far I have touched only obliquely upon the grave question of housing finance. Nearly every construction job requires a loan; nevertheless America developed no safe and satisfactory system of finance for this basic and, in the mass, tremendously large fiscal operation. There is outstanding $50,000,000,000 in real-estate mortgage loans, almost half of which cover urban home mortgages. This is the largest single category in the whole debt structure of America, exceeding by almost twice the national debt and being four times the industrial debt, yet this gigantic sum is not subject to rational control and progressive liquidation. In the recent readjustment of real-estate values nearly all interests involved suffered loss, but conservatively managed institutions of the savings and loan type, like most of those in England and a number in this country, lost comparatively little. Their relative immunity may be traced directly to two factors. Through prior saving their debtors gained thrift habits and in the main escaped carrying second mortgages; also their contracts called for steady amortization of principal. These interim payments kept the margin of value well above the principal due, in precisely the same way that deferred payments on an automobile are calculated to offset depreciation.

The drawback of the American house mortgage has been its static position. Negotiated for a relatively short period, either three or five years, it contained usually no written provision for renewal. No amortization was required, and because of this lenience the lending bank customarily made only a 50 or 60 per cent loan. As a result the bor-

SCIENCE ATTACKS THE BUILDING ENIGMA

In the Johns-Manville Research Laboratories, building materials
are experimentally impregnated at temperatures as high as
700° F. and at pressures ranging to hundreds of pounds per
square inch

A 200,000-pound Riehle Universal Testing Machine in the Johns-Manville Research Laboratories, showing an operator testing the sheer strength of an asbestos-cement board

rower was forced into the market with an already impaired security and had to pay through the nose for the remainder on second mortgages, thereby incurring a double set of legal fees and mortgage taxes.   In the recent pinch this system came under well-deserved fire.   With the passage of years mortgage security had become impaired through depreciation; borrowers had difficulty in saving their properties when mortgages matured and could not be renewed; homes that might easily have been cleared of debt, or at least put in sound condition for amortization payments in good times, either went under the red flag or were saved by desperate expedients, perhaps with government assistance.

This melancholy situation called loudly for a new procedure on home mortgages.   The first step taken in the way of cure was the creation of the Home Loan Bank system in 1932;   the next was the National Housing Act in 1934. Mr. Lewis H. Brown, president of Johns-Manville Corporation, was an important factor in drawing this act, which is having a profound influence on all private mortgage relationships.   The chief features of this measure are the elimination of the unduly burdensome second mortgage and the establishment of a single insured loan on the basis of 80 per cent of value, with a standard clause providing for amortization from the first month of occupancy.   This plan benefits both borrowers and lenders, giving the latter conservative investments always safely margined, and is likely to attract enough capital to exercise a sound and natural influence toward lower interest rates.   Johns-Manville strongly upholds the principle behind the National Housing Act, for it holds that funds for a true revival of home building must come from private sources.   All that government can do is lead off in the direction of fair and enduring standards, and this has been done.

Fundamental recovery in building awaits the general acceptance of these two lessons from recent experience. The first is that a debt is made to be repaid. This is old doctrine; your grandfather probably told it to you, but in the meantime the habit of steady repayment declined in the mortgage field. The second lesson is new to us but commonplace in Europe; this is the advantage of opening the national money market to home owners and the national mortgage market to investors by listing broadly based and easily negotiable mortgage securities on the security exchanges. Where this has been done under adequate regulation, mortgage securities have sold at highly favorable figures even in bad times.

On the question of slum clearance and the substitution of modern multiple housing, Johns-Manville takes an equally realistic and cautious view. Giant apartment houses use enormous quantities of the Corporation's products, because these meet effectively the need for low maintenance cost, low upkeep, and safety from fire, but such structures are held unlikely to drive the single family dwelling from the American heart and scene. Where such projects are the result of slum clearance, it is felt that the latter is essentially a social rather than an economic problem. Close observation of population shifts in many cities gives evidence that slums are made by slum dwellers quite as much as by neglectful landlords, corroding taxes, and scant public services. Slums can be cured by main strength at great expense, but can the slum makers be as quickly reformed? When a slum is cleared, new tenants of higher type usually invade the reconstructed area while former inhabitants move on to assist in creating another slum somewhere else. A long and necessarily slow education in better living and the proper care of modern, sanitary housing is one of the essentials of slum eradication, — which is the correct long-range objective, — whereas slum clearance as properly understood is only a temporary betterment usually missed by the very persons it is designed to help. Still, Johns-Manville is not cynical on the subject of slum clearance. It has done its share to rouse landlords toward improving their outmoded properties. Even if slum dwellers on the move create new slums, the latter may not be as foul slums as the ones left behind, and in the process some of the befoulers of decent property may have learned better ways of domestic life. The point is that Johns-Manville does not expect the impossible from any combination of government money and large-scale housing.

This discussion leaves untouched, through sheer lack of space, a broad range of subjects which have received the attention of Johns-Manville's investigators over many years. Among these are effective land utilization, sound community planning, influences of real-estate taxation, questions arising from the relationships of labor, contractors, supply dealers, realtors, architects, and manufacturers, and the vital problems of distribution, transporting, and warehousing. All that is possible within these narrow limits is to present the point of view of an enterprising corporation as it attempts to cleave through the jungle of custom and commerce which hinders the average American on his way to getting the best possible shelter for his money. To clear away the tangle is perhaps beyond the power of any single corporation; but to see the goal clearly and point the way is an act of leadership for which the entire building industry and a nation drastically in need of more and better housing may well be thankful.

MERCHANDISING LABORATORY CONTROL

*National Dairy's Sealtest Symbol, and What It Means
to Dairy Farmers and the Public*

XI

MERCHANDISING LABORATORY CONTROL

WHETHER it be the cold gray dawn or a bright sunrise, both arrive with the milk bottle. The quality of the milk in this bottle, and its presence on one's doorstep, are usually taken for granted, yet milk is one of the most delicately balanced of nature's gifts and getting pure milk from farms to city users is the biggest and most important service task performed daily by any industry.

The scale of the dairy industry is colossal. There are 25,000,000 milch cows on about 4,600,000 American farms which produce roughly 100 billion pounds of milk a year. This immense flow, less that used on farms, supplies thousands of pasteurizing and bottling plants, cheese factories, evaporating, condensing, and powdering plants, ice-cream plants, and butter factories. Production and distribution of milk and dairy products form the largest industry in the country, and dairying is far and away our largest agricultural enterprise.

Three fourths of all American farms produce milk. Take the owners and workers on these 4,600,000 farms as the base of the milk trade, add to them all persons engaged in processing and delivering milk, and you have one of the largest industrial blocs in the nation whose economic welfare is dependent upon any single commodity. To mere size is added immense social significance because of the direct relation of pure milk products to public health and the root nature of agriculture as a source of social stability.

What, then, is the present state of the dairy industry? As far back as the records run, cow numbers rise and fall in a cycle of fifteen years. Starting from a low point, the milk flow from the farms will reach its crest about seven and a half years later and then decline for an equal period. An industry of continental extent, loosely organized, manned by millions of independent operators dependent upon the slow turning of the seasons and the growth of animals, reproduces this cycle over and over; it is an economic law of nature. Consequently, when an industrial depression with reduced buying power coincides with the upward swing of the milk cycle, the results are bound to be unfavorable to American farmers.

This was the case in 1929. Only a little earlier a serious milk shortage appeared, as high consumer buying power coincided with a cyclical "low." The farm price of milk soared. Statisticians advised extreme measures for milk conservation; producers were exhorted to increase production. That seller's market started dairy farmers on an expansion programme, so that, with the decline in consumption after 1930, surplus milk crowded the market from 1930 to 1934, breaking prices and burdening dairy-farm economy.

In most businesses a steady run of losses would result in prompt curtailment of production. But in dairying or any other form of agriculture, curtailment is difficult. The herd must be kept going because it is the source of ready money, even though the long series of transactions involved in securing the weekly or monthly milk checks might net the producer little or no return at all for his time. In the lowest trough of the depression, milk ran into politics. State and federal governments attempted to rescue the dairy farmers with emergency legislation by establishing minimum farm prices for milk in various markets throughout the

Photograph by Harris & Ewing

THOMAS H. McINNERNEY
President, National Dairy Products Corporation

Ice cream is distributed in traveling ice boxes, refrigeration being
supplied either by "dry ice" or by mechanical cooling system
(*Breyer Ice Cream Company, New York and Philadelphia*)

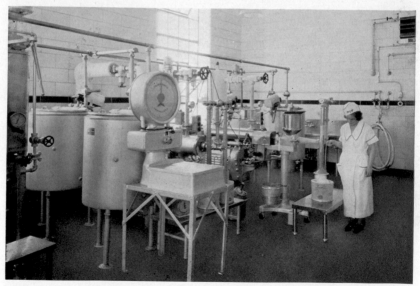

Continuous-process ice cream freezer. As the "paper" containers
are filled they go direct to the "hardening room," where below-zero
temperatures complete the freezing
(*"Fro-joy" plant of General Ice Cream Corporation, Springfield, Massachusetts*)

country. In some areas this legislation fixed both the consumer and the farm price for milk, whereupon "bootleg" milk promptly made headlines.

So vast is the dairying area, and so many are the producers, that the difficulties of any system of government control are obvious. A permanent "milk bureaucracy" could not be other than ineffective in results and burdensome to the public. The Supreme Court in the Nebbia Case upheld the jurisdiction of the New York Milk Control Board over intrastate prices; but the court followed with a decision denying the board's power to shut out of the state milk purchased beyond its borders at prices lower than those prescribed by the board. This throws the dairy industry back to the fundamental that it can protect itself only through better internal organization and closer co-operation. State government can assist it to a degree, but cannot guarantee the dairy farmer a new automobile every year. A New York dairy farmer is still at the mercy of the distressed marginal producer in another state within economic range of his chief market. Indeed, Governor Lehman of New York recently stated: —

Government for the long pull can only help and direct; it can never take the place of individual initiative nor reverse sound economic laws. It should be the policy of the state to withdraw from emergency regulation and control as soon as emergencies have passed and to foster and stimulate voluntary action on the part of farmers, dealers, and consumers to solve these problems for themselves without state intervention.

The real problem, therefore, is to bring organization among producers to a point where, through collective bargaining power, they will stand together in defense of fair prices. Indeed, one of the basic purposes in the formation of National Dairy Products Corporation, the largest dairy company in the world, was to assure milk producers a continuous market for their milk at the highest possible price. Thomas H. McInnerney, President of National Dairy, speaking before the National Coöperative Milk Producers Federation in Des Moines, Iowa, stated in 1930:—

Collective bargaining in the sale of raw material is sound and is always welcomed by fair-minded private business. Coöperative bargaining associations of farmers should be sustained.

Dairy farmers are now aware that, even at the lowest point, milk paid better returns than other farm products. The cow accounted for 15.6 per cent of total farm income in 1926; raised this to 19.5 per cent in 1929; further increased milk's leadership as a source of farm income to 23.7 per cent in 1932 (the very bottom of the agricultural depression), and even to-day, despite the substantial increase in all farm income generally, still contributed 19.4 per cent of the total amount of farm income in 1934.

Unique among industries in several respects, dairying reverses the usual rule that the big buyer gets lowest prices. In milk the exact reverse is true. The big buyer, requiring a large and regular flow to keep huge plants and distributing systems in operation, must pay highest going price to be sure of enough milk for emergencies and also for regular day-to-day variations in demand. Price advantage rests with the small buyer who can gamble on picking up whatever surplus milk is left after regular daily demand has been met. This differential can be and is overcome, in the case of large companies, by lower unit cost of operation, due to larger volume. It follows that the best interests of the large dairy companies and the best interests of dairy farmers coincide on this fundamental of steady supply at prices adequate to maintain dairy agriculture on a high plane.

We have seen in a previous article how a great milling company campaigns to increase the use of wheat, conducting merchandising and advertising drives and prosecuting scientific researches in order to increase the use of wheat products, fighting a battle for wheat growers which they are totally unable to fight for themselves, though the latter are sadly in need of increased markets for their dependable and socially necessary wares. In the dairy industry this same struggle is being waged by the large distributors with equal forethought and under conditions of even greater urgency. For milk is a highly perishable product, susceptible to contamination at all times. Milk comes to market day by day, almost hour by hour. A temporary halt in this system of supply and distribution would imperil thousands of infant lives, throw housekeeping into disorder, and unsettle the finances of millions of farmers dependent upon regular receipt of milk checks.

Under daily and hourly pressure so intense, it is beyond the power of small dealers and operators to perform more than routine merchandising functions. Upon the larger factors in the trade devolve the responsibilities of increasing milk consumption by developing new milk products and sharpening public appetite for existing products. Although the dairy industry of America leads the world in all respects, — quality and quantity of output, speed and dependability of delivery, diversity of products, and thoroughness of management, — nevertheless per capita milk consumption remains at only half the figure considered necessary to the highest level of public health. The average consumption of fluid milk, in cooking and as a beverage, is less than a pint per person per day. Nutrition scientists would double this figure. When and as their resources permit, public agencies do what they can to promote the use of milk, but consistent work in developing milk markets can be looked for only from the larger dairy distributors.

Let us see what the largest of the milk companies, National Dairy Products Corporation, has done and is doing to increase milk consumption. Concentration of capital has not gone very far in the milk trade. National Dairy handles less than 9 per cent of the total milk production of the country. There is no monopoly in milk; far from it. As in the building trade, there is not yet any single factor in the milk industry large enough to do quite all the things required for the best interests of both consumer and producer. Still, National Dairy performs services of which both the primary producers and the ultimate consumers of milk remain unaware.

On the market side, milk may be divided into two classes — fluid milk and manufacturing milk. Fluid milk — about 40 per cent of all milk sold off the farm — is the urban public's idea of milk, the milk that is brought to your doorstep in a bottle while you sleep. If fluid milk were all the milk there was, milk economics would be simple, since fluid milk commands the higher price all the way from farm to table. This is partly because it is generally sold in a restricted area, protected by local health regulations, which include inspection of farm conditions, and partly because of the expense and difficulty of transportation. If it were possible at all times for dairy farmers to receive as high a price for all their milk as they do for the part of their milk you buy in a bottle, dairying would become an agricultural gold mine.

Fluid milk enters the distributory system at a near-by rural station. There it is weighed and tested for butter fat, the constituent which gives richness. It is cooled for shipment either in 40-quart cans or in tank trucks of stainless steel or glass, the latter large thermos bottles on wheels. Arriving at the city milk plant, the milk is checked and all handling processes are inspected both by Department of Health representatives and by the company's own technicians. Laboratory tests go on continuously.

The heart of the city plant's processing is pasteurization, which kills harmful bacteria and is applied to more than 95 per cent of all city-consumed milk. Pasteurizing consists of heating milk to 143 degrees Fahrenheit for a brief period, followed by rapid cooling, and has been found so efficacious from the medical standpoint that it is favored by almost all municipal health departments.

In its progress through the plant, no human hand touches either the milk or the interior of a bottle, and exquisite care is both the rule and the practice. Dairy machinery in the better-managed plants fairly gleams with cleanliness, and research scientists search continually for ideal alloys and cleansing compounds. Housekeeping here has at its disposal all the aids that modern science can muster, for milk is crotchety stuff, easily acquiring undesirable tastes and odors and absorbing metal particles when certain conditions favor electrolysis. Through a long series of rigid tests prosecuted by National Dairy scientists in collaboration with other experts, it has been found that aluminum is superior for some uses, stainless steel for others, and chromium-nickel-iron for still others. The results of this investigation, placed at the disposal of the entire industry although financed only by its leaders, tabulate the best metal available for every piece of processing equipment used in a modern dairy. This is only one of a dozen major researches pushed by National Dairy Products along the line of advanced housekeeping,

others being aimed at selection of glass for bottle manufacturers, galvanic corrosion, and so forth. The drive for
cleanliness goes on unceasingly from dairy barn to final
delivery; and the standard of sanitation is of the laboratory
rather than the mere eye-and-nose test of common observation.

The economic significance of this "hospital" care in handling is graphically portrayed in a study made for the New
York State Milk Control Board by Dr. Leland Spencer of
Cornell University, concerning costs and profits in milk
distribution. Concisely, his findings were as follows: —

AVERAGE COSTS AND PROFITS PER QUART
19 NEW YORK CITY MILK DISTRIBUTORS
AUGUST 1933

Selling Price*	$.08651
Product Cost	.04440
Gross Spread	.04211
Operating Costs:	
Country Plants	.00469
Transportation	.00602
City Pasteurizing Plants	.00428
Containers	.00178
Delivery and Selling	.02344
General and Administrative	.00186
Total Operating Costs	.04207
Net Operating Profit	.00004
Net Other Income	.00003
Net Profit after Taxes	$.00007

*This is the average price these companies received per quart for all their milk sold
retail and wholesale, or in the form of cream, butter, cheese, etc.

Not many persons would believe that a milk company in any city would have to sell 143 quarts of milk to make one cent, or that a quart of milk could be delivered for less than the United States Government charges for delivering mail of less weight and bulk.

So much for the river of milk which flows to your door. An even larger river rising at the same source flows into factories to emerge as butter, cheese, and other types of milk products. Some dairy farmers have no fluid market, producing only for manufacturing purposes. In this broad competition the determining price factor is cost of production in the most favored area, Wisconsin and southern Minnesota, because milk products can be shipped from one end of the country to another. Butter alone uses about half of all milk sold commercially off the farm. Therefore the farm price for this "surplus" of manufacturing milk is primarily determined by the selling price of butter. The law of supply and demand fixes this price in a national market. If butter sells at retail for 35 cents a pound, it is obvious that the price the farmer can receive for the $10\frac{1}{2}$ quarts of milk required to make one pound of butter cannot exceed three cents a quart, even were there no churning and marketing costs. For milk sold in a bottle, however, the farmer receives roughly twice as much as he does for milk sold as butter. Only by means of this price differential is it possible to use all farm milk and prepare it for consumption at prices which consumers can pay. With this situation governing, farmers who produce primarily for fluid consumption must sell their surplus milk at a price in relation to the going price on butter.

Major outlets for manufacturing milk are butter, cheese, and ice cream. Butter making and cheese making are among the most ancient of household arts, while ice-cream making is so new that the ice-cream soda received its first large-scale introduction to the public at the World's Fair in Chicago in 1893. Since the beginning of the present century all three have advanced to new standards and greater volume as the result of factory production, scientific quality control, and effective merchandising.

Fifty years ago, for instance, it was still difficult to get good butter unless one had direct contact with an exceptionally cleanly farm. Production went on entirely unsupervised and in many cases without even a faint regard for sanitary precautions. Lack of refrigeration made for early spoilage. Needless to say, quality has been so improved that butter no longer worries housewives.

National Dairy is well represented in the butter industry and is the largest single manufacturer of ice cream. One of the Breyer ice-cream plants is the largest in the world. National Dairy has pioneered with its ice-cream divisions in quality control, and aided materially in solving distributing and merchandising problems. Ice cream, cheese, butter, and miscellaneous by-product sales represent more than half of National Dairy's sales dollar.

In the important cheese trade, which markets more than 500,000,000 pounds and is steadily growing, National Dairy also has most distinguished representation: Kraft-Phenix Cheese Corporation. Kraft is the leader, not only in the manufacture and distribution of domestic cheese, but also in the importation of foreign cheeses into the United States. Kraft manufactures in thirty-eight states of the Union and in five foreign countries. It markets approximately one hundred varieties of packaged cheese and closely allied cheese foods belonging to fifteen distinctive cheese families, eight varieties of mayonnaise and other salad spreads and dressings, in addition to malted milk and several whey

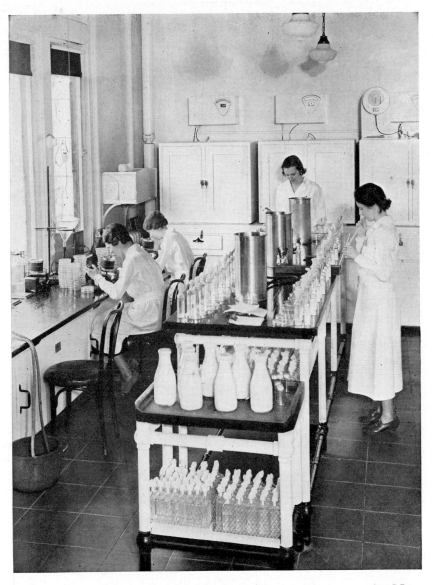

One of the laboratories of Sheffield Farms Company in New York, where bacteria content, acidity, and butter-fat content are carefully checked to ensure milk of highest quality

Where flavor development begins — Swiss "wheels" in their "salt baths" at the Kraft plant in Antigo, Wisconsin. The "wheels" next go to man-made "caves" for several months of curing

Thousands of fast refrigerated trucks keep dealers' stocks of Kraft cheese, salad dressings, mayonnaise, and other Kraft products strictly fresh

by-products under trade names. By pioneering colorfully in packaging and advertising, Kraft has been the energizer of the whole cheese trade, rousing housewives' interest in cheese and lifting per capita cheese consumption by more than 50 per cent in the last two decades. James L. Kraft started to modernize the cheese business in Chicago in 1904, with a one-horse wagon and $65 in capital; to-day the Kraft company's business is international in scope.

Of the many forward steps taken by his company in revolutionizing the cheese business, Mr. Kraft considers three decisive. First, prompt delivery of packaged cheeses at their best. Every day Kraft trucks move from the central warehouses to wholesalers, and others move from the wholesalers to retailers, thereby providing fresh stocks all along the line. Second, consistent research in the chemistry of milk, which resulted about 1915 in the successful blending of pasteurized cheese standardized as to taste, purity, and nutritional value. Third, the selling of cheese in sealed, air-tight containers. Processing improvements created superior and dependable goods; packaging improvements commended them to storekeepers and housewives by reason of economy in storage and use. Package sizes range from the five-pound loaf down to the small rectangles of Philadelphia Cream Cheese, a Kraft leader.

Another volume development was the addition of mayonnaise and salad dressings. Kraft's expanding distribution system could accommodate another line of packaged table goods. Kraft laboratories after long experiment provided both improved recipes and production machinery, Kraft advertising gained a steady market, and to-day these non-cheese items bulk large in the company's turnover. Similar considerations brought Kraft into the milk-candy field with Kraft caramels.

Whatever Kraft does, it does largely and boldly. It now has at Antigo, Wisconsin, the largest Swiss-cheese plant in the world. Its malted-milk plant at Wausau, Wisconsin, also leads in size and modernity. Kraft took cheese making South by establishing plants and stations from Virginia to Texas. By providing a market for Southern milk in an area which had never before produced cheese, Kraft's Southern march is contributing to both the industrial and the agricultural development of that region, just as its earlier expansion did in California, Idaho, and Montana.

In number of laboratories and their geographical spread, no industry is richer than the dairy industry, but the majority of these laboratories are occupied with products control rather than fundamental research. One of National Dairy's first tasks, after its organization in 1923, was to establish at Baltimore a well-equipped laboratory to do for each of its associated companies whatever they were unable to do for themselves, and to study thoroughly the complex chemistry of milk. The publications of these laboratories cover a multitude of technical subjects reported on in special bulletins and in scientific journals. However, after years of fundamental work along this line, Thomas H. McInnerney, President of National Dairy, became convinced that a closer tie was needed between laboratory results and field practice in the widespread and highly decentralized organization which he formed and continues dynamically to lead.

These facts appeared self-evident. Milk in the bottle, as in several other forms, never has enjoyed the benefit of a strong champion on the national stage. Other food products had long been advertised under trade names in national magazines, and such brand advertising helped manufacturers of like goods indirectly, even though they were not advertisers. No dairy company was using the immense and effective power of the magazine press, so influential to domestic sales and to the cultivation of good will among future buyers, in behalf of the most necessary and healthful of all foods — milk.

To advertise milk and milk products nationally had its special difficulties. The operating companies of National Dairy are captained largely by men who created them, for milk distribution on the modern plane is a rather new business in which proud family names still bulk large. National Dairy desired to reënforce these local loyalties, each of which had its commercial value. Also, owing to the local character of milk regulations, differing standards and customs prevailed in different cities. At the same time, it was perceived that if definite quality specifications could be established and maintained the dairy industry would reach a new dignity and prestige, beneficial particularly to the dairy farmers of the country.

With this goal fixed, National Dairy looked for precedents and found one in the history of its great New York subsidiary, Sheffield Farms Co., Inc., which delivers daily 1,000,000 quarts of milk. Sheffield has many claims to leadership in the industry. It was the first dairy in America to employ the pasteurizing process and the first to establish a complete protection for the consumer on bottled milk, a service involving its own farm inspection programme and progressively higher standards in transport, processing, and bottling. Early in its history Sheffield had established premium milk grades.

Just as Sheffield set the pace in New York City, so National Dairy concluded that it could proceed along that line on a broader basis. To its central laboratories, reincorporated under the name Sealtest System Laboratories,

Inc., was assigned the task of fixing quality specifications, checking daily reports, supervising individual laboratories through a zone control system, inspecting plants, granting permits for the use of the Sealtest symbol, and checking by consistent laboratory tests the findings from frequent visits of staff members among dairy plants. Operations thus rigidly controlled were given the right to use the Sealtest symbol on their products. The first broad application of this new system was made in the ice-cream field, which lends itself particularly well to standardization. In this presentation National Dairy sank itself almost out of sight, stressing the scores of trade names built up by its subsidiaries and celebrating its unity of purpose only through the Sealtest symbol. For the first time ice-cream advertising found a place on the home reading table. Sales results proved so favorable that doubters in the great National Dairy family of corporations began to seek the Sealtest symbol for other products. At present some National Dairy companies are using the Sealtest symbol on milk and other products, and this use will broaden greatly. No National Dairy unit is permitted to use the Sealtest symbol until it has satisfied the scientist-officers of the Sealtest organization, and, once in the charmed circle, it must maintain the standards established.

In the main the Sealtest plan is designed to fix as an irreducible minimum the highest standards ruling in each locality, and then to lift quality operations as far above that standard as the economics of the situation permit. Any cost a business assumes to improve quality is always a sound investment. For instance, when Sheffield first developed a superior quality milk, it gained and held to this day an extremely large number of customers who desired and were willing to pay for this special milk.

The Sealtest symbol means that efficient dairy housekeeping has been taught to local staffs by lecture and instruction, that it is enforced by inspectors with laboratory training, that both raw and processed materials have passed high tests on all valid points. Each department is rated separately; there is no blanket dispensation given to all products of a factory producing more than one kind or grade of food, but each product must deserve Sealtest distinction in its own right.

National Dairy executives feel that Sealtest merchandising, soundly based on selling the housewife quality dairy products, will champion the worth-while cause of increased milk consumption.

This accomplishment would mean increased purchasing power for dairy farmers and a high level of public health, thoughts basic to Thomas H. McInnerney when he organized National Dairy only a little more than ten years ago.

GRINDING AS THE COMMON DENOMINATOR OF MASS PRODUCTION

Norton Abrasives at Work in Industry

XII

GRINDING AS THE COMMON DENOMINATOR OF MASS PRODUCTION

THIS series on twelve great fabricating industries began on the note of Precision and Perspective. The first chapter, on General Motors, bore that phrase for a title. Each of the subsequent chapters presented various phases of the relationship between precise manufacturing methods and the satisfaction of public needs through improved goods and services. The series ends, with this article on the Norton Company, on the same note of precision and perspective. Purposely this article has been held for the final position because Norton products — abrasives in many forms — enter directly or indirectly into all the complicated fabricating and processes which have been discussed.

Grinding is a common denominator of refined fabrication. In metals it has become the essential element of machine practice, both in the creation of better machines for all lines of production and in the operation of those machines in the quantity output of consumers' goods. The automobile, steel, electrical, and paper industries, in their later phases, all owe to abrasives a large part of their ability to supply quality goods at low cost, while the efficiency of the other industries studied depends largely on machine equipment ground and finished to better than hairline precision. The shining stainless pipes of the modern dairy, the massive steel beds on which plate glass is carried under the polishing pads, the trim machines which shape and test tin cans in endless procession, the presses which give shape to asbestos products, the mighty valves which control the passage of oil through the refinery, and the steel rolls which turn wheat into flour — all these take shape and depend for repair upon grinding machines and grinding wheels. There is scarcely an aspect of modern industry which could function at its present speed and effectiveness if grinding had failed to advance with other branches of applied science.

The use of abrasives is as old as the hills which provided primitive warriors with stones on which to grind their arrowheads. You use abrasives when you bring a lead pencil to a point on a piece of sandpaper. Hardly a dwelling or a piece of furniture stands in the world that has not felt the smoothing touch of an abrasive. But the natural abrasives in the hand of man could not cope with all the grinding tasks set up by the delicate requirements of modern industry as it developed increasingly hard materials and advanced to new standards of precision. In this transition the Norton Company of Worcester, Massachusetts, through its research, inventions, and policies, has earned a proud place in American industrial history by pioneering in the manufacture of artificial abrasives and their machine use at high speeds.

The centre of this great business, now basic and world-wide in scope, remains in Worcester, where it took root many years ago as a pottery. F. B. Norton, however, was a potter willing to flirt with a new idea; and when one of his employees suggested making a grinding wheel out of emery, in 1873, he agreed to back the effort. After six years of trial and error, finally crowned with success, the Norton emery wheel came to market. Another six years and Norton Emery Wheel Company was formed, just fifty years ago. With Mr. Norton at that time were John

GEORGE N. JEPPSON
Vice President and Treasurer

ALDUS C. HIGGINS
President, Norton Company

CHARLES L. ALLEN
Chairman of the Board

In the stone industry abrasives have an important place in cutting and finishing granite and marble, and for pressure blasting in monumental work

Logs of the forest are converted into wood pulp by manufactured abrasive pulpstone, the largest of which weigh approximately ten tons

Jeppson, master craftsman, who almost single-handed mixed, fired, trued, and sold the early output, and Charles L. Allen, bookkeeper, later General Manager for forty-eight years, then President and now Chairman of the Board. This group was joined by two professors of science from Worcester Polytechnic Institute, Milton P. Higgins and George I. Alden, who gave the Norton Company the benefit of their trained minds and accurate knowledge while continuing their teaching careers, and later became active in Company affairs. Their influence brought Norton into the orbit of applied science at a time when most American industries were still following rule-of-thumb methods, and left with the institution a tradition of exact methods. In 1886 the Company built at Barber's Crossing, north of Worcester, a modest building forty-two feet by one hundred, which still stands as part of the vast Norton factories on the present site.

Scientific aid proved timely, for revolutionary changes were in train for all American industry and particularly for the abrasive arts. By the end of the century the possibilities of the natural grits, emery and corundum, had been exhausted. The industry turned to two types of artificial abrasives, both products of the electric furnace. First in the field was silicon carbide, made from silica sand, coke, and sawdust. Possessing hard, sharp, though somewhat brittle crystals, it was suited to grinding the materials low in tensile strength. Its limitations soon became apparent. The next great gift to the industry was an aluminum oxide abrasive, produced by fusing the mineral bauxite, a Norton development which was trade-named Alundum. Manufacture of the abrasive which was to become so successful in the working of steel and steel alloys began at Niagara Falls in 1901.

About the turn of the century occurred two seemingly unrelated happenings which were to join forces with tremendous vigor. The automobile, after several false starts, swung into its stride with the initial commercial success of Olds Motor Works at Detroit. At the same time Charles H. Norton was designing his first cylindrical grinding machine at Providence, Rhode Island. He found a willing backer in the grinding wheel company at Worcester and in 1900 the Norton Grinding Machine Company was established.

Here was precisely the medium the automobile industry needed to shape interchangeable parts to close measurements from tough stock at low cost, an abrasive that could stand the gaff and, properly bonded, grind the common metals down to a thousandth of an inch, thereby eliminating expensive lathe work. Here, too, was a machine on which grinding wheels of greater breadth could be mounted and moved transversely, under accurate and mechanically controlled guidance, across securely held metals. From the start the combination of Alundum wheels and Norton machines was ideal for grinding the all-important crankshafts and camshafts. For years leading automobile makers sent camshafts to Worcester to be ground; but gradually, as Norton machines and wheels became more common and more mechanics mastered the art of grinding, this practice lapsed, until to-day every automobile factory has in its shops employees equal to the most delicate tasks required.

Norton has never been content to rest on its priority in past performances, or to attempt quick profit at the expense of industry as a whole. Its superior knowledge of the grinding art was early placed at the service of manufacturers and mechanics, and education of the men behind the machines the country over has always been one of its chief concerns. Norton has for years presented technical lectures and demonstrations in industrial towns and cities so that a more intimate and comprehensive knowledge of abrasives and grinding-machine manufacture might be passed along to supervisors and operators interested in their application. That is perhaps one reason why Norton innovations encounter so little resistance in the shops among men naturally conservative.   Here is registered Norton's faith that every improvement in grinding widens the field for abrasives and that this ever-broadening use more than makes up in the long run for decrease in immediate sales caused by wheels that last longer and do more work.

Artificial abrasives are born in the electric furnace. Norton established its first electric furnace plant in 1901 at Niagara Falls, where cheap current was available, and its second across the Niagara River in Chippawa, Ontario, in 1910. The Chippawa plant is now the largest electric-furnace operation in the world for the production of abrasives, with an annual capacity of 50,000 tons of Alundum and Crystolon abrasives.

In this great plant one sees bauxite ore being transformed into Alundum abrasive in long rows of Higgins water-cooled, arc-type pot furnaces, invented in 1904 by Aldus C. Higgins, now President of the Norton Company. Mr. Higgins received the John Scott medal for this basic improvement, which made the steel furnace capable of holding and utilizing heats which otherwise would have destroyed the shell. Out of these furnaces come huge white-hot ingots, the core of which is almost pure aluminum oxide, ready, after cooling, for granular division into the various abrasive sizes.

Crystolon, or silicon carbide, the other standard abrasive for high-speed work, is made in resistance furnaces from sand, coke, and sawdust. The sand is almost pure silica;

the coke, source of carbon, is the best grade obtainable; the sawdust is hardwood residue from lumber camps, and effective chiefly in lightening the mix to permit easy escape for gases. Under electric heat the mix cooks long and thoroughly, shrinking the while; and when the core has been cleared of sinter the humble coke and sand have been transformed into a mass of iridescent crystals, running from light blue to black-green, which in the course of time will be buffing leather, grinding metals and wood pulp, smoothing automobile finishes, and cutting granite.

Ever since Charles H. Norton built his first cylindrical grinder in 1900, a feat which years later was recognized by the award of the coveted John Scott medal, the Norton Company has been building, in the best New England tradition, machinery for use in the abrasive arts. For a century Worcester has enjoyed a reputation for machine design and construction and Worcester workers have been nurtured in a tradition of machine precision. In the beginning the Norton grinding machine was an important element in opening the market for Norton abrasives; where other abrasive manufacturers could offer only the materials for the new grinding technique, Norton offered both materials and machines, thereby clearing the path to increased efficiency at one sweep. At once a close and enduring relation arose between Norton and the users of Norton abrasives. Through the years Norton leadership grew naturally out of this union of machine building and abrasive production.

Norton's first grinding machine removed one cubic inch of metal per minute, with greater accuracy than ever before known. Both in quantity and in quality of work it more than met all the inventor's claim for economy, becoming a cutting tool as well as a finishing tool. Since then Norton machines have been developed to the point where capacity for removing metal has reached twelve cubic inches per minute, while accuracy of grinding has risen from a thousandth of an inch to a fraction of a ten-thousandth. Divide a cross section of a hair of your head thirty times and a Norton grinder will match that minute measurement in repeat operations. The trend has been away from the original general-purpose grinder toward specialized machines to cope with the growing refinement in shop practices; at present Norton makes approximately one hundred machines of various sizes and types. Among recent developments are lapping machines, which bring ground surfaces to still further smoothness by removing the microscopic marks left by grinding wheels.

Throughout the entire industrial world, but particularly in the iron-working industries, the grinding machine has become indispensable to quantity manufacture in a degree incomprehensible to the hurrying public that daily uses its products. It is one of the decisive hidden factors in the low cost and high output of machine tools, automobiles, locomotives, wood-working machinery, automatic refrigerators, armament, printing presses, cash registers, typewriters, adding machines, linotypes and monotypes, and agricultural equipment from simple hand tools to mammoth combination reapers and binders. The automobile industry, dependent for its amazing advances upon complete interchangeability of machined parts, could hardly have reached its present volume but for the steady increase in accuracy at low cost made possible by the grinding machine. No machine development of the past century has affected more profoundly the efficiency of manufacturing precision goods, and through them the way of life of the people.

Norton research, now represented by three staffs, has played a master rôle in the development of abrasives ever since the industrial developments of the turn of the century brought precision grinding into new importance. The Norton conception of research is eminently practical, in natural reaction to industry's unremitting pressure for better grinding tools and materials. An example was the demand which the automobile industry raised when the practice of buffing solder placed labor in danger of lead poisoning in an industry highly cautious against that menace. In response, the Behr-Manning division research staff developed waterproof grinding disks, in order that dangerous dust could be wet down and washed away by water at every point in the operation.

Another research rescue by Norton followed the development of the so-called cemented carbides. Tools made of these new products were of superior hardness and cut extremely well; but they were difficult to condition. Norton met this challenge by creating the diamond (bort) wheel, the abrasive consisting of crushed diamonds of commercial grade. These wheels immensely widened the field of utility for cemented carbides; in addition, their use penetrated other industrial processes of most precise nature, rendering commonplace certain refined operations in grinding which had never been commercially possible before.

The above were special quests, undertaken to relieve distressed customers and meet the more demanding requirements of advancing industry. An equally important class of research problems arise through the chronic dissatisfaction of research scientists with existing products and processes. At first these may be general quests, originating with an individual's idea that improvement is possible; but as the

Roll grinding in the steel industry produces foil; strip steel for razor blades; sheet steel for tin cans, oil pipe lines, automobile bodies; and structural steel shapes

Interchangeability of machined parts such as crankshafts and camshafts, and some two hundred other parts of the automobile, depends on cylindrical grinding, commercially possible to a precision of .00025 inch

The polishing wheel used in the production of agricultural implements such as shovels, hoes, harrows, and ploughs is coated with Norton abrasives

In the glass industry abrasives play an important part in the finishing and beveling of such large-volume items as automobile windshields

search proceeds it involves teamwork of all members and sections.   In each branch of science experts carry the search along until what was at first merely an idea has been materialized, manufactured, tested, and sold.

A new product discovered through this indirect approach is Norbide, the trade name for Norton boron carbide, a compound of such extreme hardness that it ranks next to the diamond in the hardness scale.   The research staff at Chippawa, constantly experimenting with various carbon compounds in their electric furnaces, found new ways of combining carbon and boric acid.   Norbide is making its way in powdered or grain form as lapping material for tasks requiring extreme precision, and in moulded forms, such as nozzles for sandblasting, where utmost hardness is needed to resist intense wear.   However, no one knows how far any new material will go in industry once the formula has been found for its successful manufacture. The artificial abrasives which are now the foundation of the grinding art were once highly expensive; but with increasing demand ways were found to cheapen them until they could become the backbone of quantity production. This may be equally true of Norton's new find under changing conditions.

More meaningful from the standpoint of immediate acceptance on a broad scale, because it could be applied promptly to large use, is the now famous "B" bond.

Norton's experience with bonds ran back fifty years, to the pioneer days when grinding wheels occasionally burst under stress, and extreme precautions for safety marked the rise of the company.   In the meantime Norton had developed and adopted shellac, silicate of soda, Bakelite, and rubber bonds for special purposes, but the standard bond for grinding wheels remained vitrified bond, a clay bond which under the intense heat of firing turns to glass, tough, highly resistant glass capable of holding abrasive grains under tremendous stresses. These clay glasses offer a wider range of materials and qualities than the other bonding materials; if the ideal materials existed they would probably be discovered in this field. Before these were found, however, between two hundred and three hundred different glasses were made and studied until at last the correct formula was reached and industry was given a superior cutting tool.

In this long search all sections of the Norton laboratories coöperated. The microscopic section studied glass samples with the petrographic microscope, which reveals the shape and nature of crystals, identifies the elements in the compound, and shows the distribution of the elements more clearly than chemical analysis. Physical chemists ran qualitative tests; industrial physicists studied the new bond with relation to the plant problems of mixing, refining, and firing. Ceramic engineers considered the application of the new products in factory processes; mechanical engineers experimented with the machine phases of the problem. When the time came to put "B" bond into production, Norton followed its usual procedure of keeping the development research in control of those particular factory processes until the new materials had been manufactured, shipped, and tested in use in the production plants of its customers. Not until the worth of the new bond has been proved up to the hilt under widely varying conditions in actual commercial work is a Norton innovation left to the usual factory control staff. In this case five years elapsed between the conception of this research problem and its materialization as a fully tested and standardized Norton product definitely proved to be dependable and superior in grinding precision.

"B" bond overcomes undesirable features which unfit ordinary vitrified bonds for precise tool and cutter work — chemical reactions which occur during burning in the kiln and physical strains which develop during subsequent cooling. These affect adversely the internal arrangement of the grains, or abrasive cutting points of the wheel, and also the strength — uniformity of the bond. Gripping each individual abrasive grain uniformly, "B" bond makes for slow wearing and cool, free cutting.

A grinding wheel may weigh anything from ten tons to ten grams, and its work may be anything from grinding logs into pulp to slotting a fountain pen. But, whatever the size or material, all wheels consist of three factors — the abrasive which removes the material, the bond which holds the abrasive in place, and the pores or air spaces which permit the chips to escape during the grinding operation. The relation of these three factors determines the serviceability of the tool both in quality and quantity of work and in length of life. If their relationship changes even slightly during stress of work, the result is something less than perfection. Variations were not important in the early days of industrial grinding; but with the growing use of harder and more expensive steels, and the pressure toward greater accuracy, every grinding improvement became a vital step in industrial efficiency.

Control of structure is another contribution of Norton research, through which the actual spacing of the abrasive grains — the tiny cutting particles — is accurately regulated. Each spacing of the grains — each structure — is designated by a definite symbol and can be specified and duplicated at any time, just as grain size and grade are specified. The result is ability to provide customers with wheels more rigidly standardized than was possible before.

Once a Norton product has been standardized for production and sale, its control passes from research to the general inspection staff, which continues the routine work of inspection along lines laid down by research, referring to the latter department only special cases. The research department, however, maintains a check of all Norton products made in the foreign plants. From the Canadian plant at Hamilton, Ontario; the French at La Courneuve, near Paris; the British plant at Welwyn Garden City, near London; the German plant at Wesseling, near Cologne; and the Italian plant at Corsico, near Milan, samples are sent to Worcester for elaborate tests in order that Norton products may be kept to rigid quality the world over, establishing the same confidence among foreign users as at home.

Norton's foreign plants, situated in the great industrial nations, are becoming vital links in a world-wide system. Each is the answer to a commercial necessity arising out of tariffs, variations in exchange values, quota systems, or some other factor interfering with the flow of American-made abrasive products in foreign trade. Norton would have preferred to keep all this work at home, but under present world conditions this is impossible. The products from the Norton abrasive plant are transferred to Worcester, where they are crushed to commercial grain sizes and separated into various sizes for further manufacture both at home and abroad. The finished material of the Chippawa plant becomes in turn the raw material of the Worcester plant, and part of that volume, as semi-finished material, goes abroad to become the raw material of overseas operations. Part of the work has been saved for American labor, and at the same time each of the leading foreign industrial countries is assured of safe domestic production of abrasives, a matter of such moment to industrial welfare and national defense that abrasive manufacture would have gone forward there in any case, whether Norton had coöperated or not.

As the Norton Company advanced from emery toward the more competent artificial abrasives, it shortened its name; and through astute national advertising has managed to make the word Norton synonymous with abrasives. To give complete abrasive service, Norton entered allied fields through combination with Behr-Manning Corporation at Troy, New York, and the Pike Manufacturing Company, now the Norton Pike Company, situated at Littleton, New Hampshire.

Behr-Manning makes sandpapers and other coated abrasive products in bewildering variety, using as its abrasives flint (really quartz), emery, garnet (from the Adirondacks), Alundum and Crystolon grains (supplied by Norton). Itself a merger of the Herman Behr and Manning interests, this company maintains decisive leadership in its field. In a plant filled with originally designed machinery, the chief exhibit is the electro-coating or "Lightning" process, by means of which high electrical charges automatically sort abrasive grains into even spacing at minute distances from each other and draw them into the bonding glue in the upright position where they perform best. Until one visits Behr-Manning, he never dreams how complicated the abrasive business is, even with as apparently simple a commodity as sandpaper.

The Norton Pike Company can trace its ancestry back to 1823, when the Pike Manufacturing Company was established for the purpose of converting New Hampshire rock into scythestones. As time passed, products made of natural stones found in half a dozen different states and several foreign countries were manufactured to meet specific sharpening requirements. Of these, the most distinctive products are those made from the Arkansas novaculites, used for sharpening surgeons' and engravers' tools. With the introduction of artificial abrasives, the widely known India oilstones, made from Norton Alundum abrasive, were brought on the market, followed by others made from the silicon carbide abrasive Crystolon. Thus all abrasive demands from the hardware trade and the household user have been included in the Norton line.

In addition to these standard products, Norton markets a broad range of abrasive goods in other forms. For the building trade it manufactures non-slip floors, tiles, and treads in a wide variety of colors and designs, providing sure traction. Or it will sell you Alundum aggregate and tell you how to mix it with terrazzo and cement for walkways where traffic is heavy. Its porous plates, practically indestructible filters, are used not only in laboratory work but in the activated sludge type of sewerage disposal plants. Abrasive grains for polishing can be bought in all sizes. Norton bricks and sticks are available for all manner of cleaning, smoothing, and polishing jobs. The high resistance of Norton abrasives to heat makes Norton refractories available for many furnace operations beyond the range of ordinary firebrick. The huge Norton pulpstones are converting logs of the forest into pulp for newsprint. These materials represent as yet only a fraction of Norton's production, but they are part of the Norton plan to anticipate market needs by research and development, providing complete coverage in abrasives even though new products are brought out in advance of effective demand.

These are among the tangible factors in the manufacture of Norton abrasives. But in industry, as in life itself, intangibles are equally important. We have seen, in other chapters of this series, how great corporations function in welfare work, employee education, labor-relations plans, insurance protection, following lines of thought and action directed toward individual improvement and community betterment.

Norton also has done its share in these directions, but it has succeeded better than most in avoiding both complexity and paternalism in these group relationships. It has relied chiefly on keeping alive and effective under modern conditions and increasing size the spirit which was so strikingly evident in its early days, when bosses were artisans as well as employers and when every workman knew what everyone else in the business was doing to advance the general welfare of the group. A pleasant custom of celebrating festivals together comes down from a time when the labor staff was small enough to gather with management around a table for Christmas dinner. Growth of numbers rendering this impossible, Norton now gives a Christmas turkey to every employee — 4000 employees, 4000 turkeys. Through a service director the company guides work in education, recreation, sanitation, dental care, safety, health, and nursing, and coöperates with employee groups interested in housing, insurance, mutual loans, agriculture, photography, and sports.

The Norton spirit — the intangible behind the tangibles of production — is materialized artistically in Norton Hall, in the heart of the big Worcester plant. On the walls of Norton Hall are a series of ten impressive murals by Arthur Covey, each panel illustrating labor's part in the rise of the abrasive industry. And occupying the end of the room is a graphic tree of Norton history, containing the names of all the men who, from bench to desk, contributed outstandingly to the beginnings and rise of the company. There is preserved, for the eye of future generations of Norton men and women, recognition of the part played by personalities and loyalties in the rise of this enterprise to leadership in the intricate business of making abrasives a key factor in America's industrial advance.